James Payn

Draft of the Prison Law

James Payn

Draft of the Prison Law

ISBN/EAN: 9783744758932

Printed in Europe, USA, Canada, Australia, Japan

Cover: Foto ©ninafisch / pixelio.de

More available books at **www.hansebooks.com**

DRAFT OF

THE PRISON LAW.

PREPARED BY

The Commissioners of Statutory Revision.

(To be Submitted to the Legislature of 1899.)

PRELIMINARY NOTE.

The Prison Law is submitted herewith as a proposed chapter of the general laws. It contains a revision of all general laws relating to county jails, penitentiaries, state reformatories for male adults and state prisons. All provisions respecting the powers and duties of officers of such institutions and the care, treatment and employment of prisoners confined therein are included.

The provisions of the present law relating to county jails and prisoners confined therein are now found in the county law (L. 1892. ch. 686), §§ 94–103 and the code of civil procedure, §§ 110-189. These sections are transferred to this law and arranged in articles thereof without material change. The county penitentiaries are established and controlled pursuant to special statutes severally applicable to each of them. We have not attempted to adapt any general scheme of mangement to these institutions. The statutes generally applicable to all such institutions are included without change, except as noted at the end of each section. (See Article IV.)

Chapter 711 of the Laws of 1887 provides for the management of the Elmira reformatory. We have revised this law, making it applicable to the Eastern reformatory at Napanoch when ready for occupancy. Some changes are suggested in the revision which are explained and commented upon in the notes. (See Article V.)

The state prisons are now managed and controlled pursuant to Part IV, chap. 2, title II, of the Revised Statutes, as amended by L. 1889, chap. 382. This part of the Revised Statutes is included in articles of the proposed revision. The changes made are, for the most part, verbal and do not affect the system of administration now in force. The organization, powers and duties of the State Commission of Prisons are set forth in Article XXII of the proposed law. This article is a re-enactment of L. 1895, ch. 1026. The changes made are noted at the end of the sections.

The revision also embraces the provisions of the present statutes relating to the execution of the death penalty, the employment of prisoners in penitentiaries and state prisons, the manufacture of supplies therein for the use of the state and the political divisions thereof, the discipline and commutation for good conduct of prisoners and reprieves, commutations and pardons by the governor.

Each article contains at the beginning thereof a brief note explaining its scope and application. Under each section is a reference to the section of the present law from which it is derived, with a statement of the changes made, if any, and the reasons therefor.

CHARLES Z. LINCOLN,

WILLIAM H. JOHNSON,

A. JUDD NORTHRUP,

Commissioners of Statutory Revision.

ALBANY, N. Y., *September* 15, 1898.

AN ACT

In relation to prisons, constituting chapter fifteen of the general laws.

The People of the State of New York, represented in Senate and Assembly, do enact as follows:

CHAPTER XV OF THE GENERAL LAWS.

THE PRISON LAW.

Article   I. Penal institutions; definitions. (§§ 1-12.)

II. Jails. (§§ 20-50.)

III. Confinement of civil prisoners; jail liberties. (§§ 60-85.)

IV. Penitentiaries. (§§ 90-96.)

V. Reformatories. (§§ 100-127.)

VI. State prisons; officers. (§§ 140-157.)

VII. State prisons; finances and property. (§§ 160-174.)

VIII. State prisons; sentence, reception, transportation and transfer of prisoners. (§§ 180-188.)

IX. State prisons; special provisions relative to care and treatment of prisoners. (§§ 200-208.)

X. State prisons; board of parole; parole of prisoners. (§§ 220-229.)

XI. State prisons; prisoners under sentence of death; execution of sentence. (§§ 240-249.)

Article XII. State prison for women. (§§ 250-257.)

XIII. Dannemora hospital for insane convicts. (§§ 260-274.)

XIV. Classification and employment of prisoners. (§§ 280-288.)

XV. Manufacture of supplies in penal institutions for use of state and political divisions thereof. (§§ 300-311.)

XVI. Conduct of manufacturing industries in state prisons. (§§ 320-331.)

XVII. Compensation of prisoners in state prisons and penitentiaries. (§§ 340-343.)

XVIII. Discipline and commutations for good conduct. (§§ 350-361.)

XIX. Reprieves, commutations and pardons by the governor. (§§ 370-375.)

XX. Miscellaneous provisions. (§§ 380-385.)

XXI. State commission of prisons. (§§ 390-398.)

XXII. Laws repealed; when to take effect. (§§ 400-401.)

ARTICLE I.

PENAL INSTITUTIONS; DEFINITIONS.

Section 1. Short title.

2. Definition of penal institution.

3. Classification.

4. Jails.

5. Penitentiaries.

6. Reformatories.

Section 7. State prisons.

    8. Warden.

    9. Superintendent.

    10. Commission.

    11. Prisoner.

    12. Political division.

[General note.—This article contains definitions of certain terms commonly used in subsequent articles of the bill, and are inserted so that a shorter term may be used for all that it signifies. The statute is thus divested of many useless words.

We have also classified the several penal institutions treated in this chapter and declared the purpose for which each of such institutions is maintained.]

§ 1. Short title.—This chapter shall be known as the prison law.

§ 2. Definition of penal institution.—The term "penal institution," when used in this chapter, means an institution used, wholly or in part, for the confinement of persons convicted of crime, held awaiting trial or the action of a grand jury, detained as witnesses or as civil prisoners, except institutions of a correctional or reformatory character used solely for the imprisonment of females convicted of a misdemeanor, or of children under the age of sixteen years, when convicted of either a misdemeanor or a felony.

[New. By article VIII, § 11, of the constitution, the state commission of prisons is vested with the power of visitation and inspection of all "institutions used for the detention of sane adults charged with or convicted of crime, or detained as witnesses or debtors." It is designed to include in this chapter of the general laws institutions which are subject to the visitation of the state commission of prisons.]

§ 3. Classification.—For the purposes of this chapter the following are treated as penal institutions.

1. Jails.

2. Penitentiaries.

3. Reformatories.

4. State prisons.

[New.]

§ 4. Jails.—Jails are established and maintained by counties for the confinement or detention of:

1. Persons charged with crime, and committed for trial, examination, or to await the action of a grand jury.

2. Persons convicted and sentenced to imprisonment therein for an offense other than a felony.

3. Persons awaiting transportation under a sentence of imprisonment in another penal institution.

4. Persons duly committed to secure their attendance as witnesses in a criminal case.

5. Persons duly committed for a contempt or upon a civil process.

[This section is derived from County Law, § 90, which prescribes the use of county jails.

Subdivision 1 of the above section is the same as subdivision 2 of such § 90, except that the words " or to await the action of a grand jury" are added.

Subdivision 2 is the same as the first clause of subdivision 4. Subdivision 3 corresponds to the last clause of subdivision 4. Subdivisions 4 and 5 are the same as subdivisions 1 and 3 of the present § 90.]

§ 5. Penitentiaries.—Penitentiaries are established and maintained by counties for the confinement of persons convicted of:

1. Misdemeanors.

2. Felonies, where the sentences imposed are for terms of less than one year.

[New.]

§ 6. Reformatories.—Reformatories, for the purposes of this chapter, are state institutions for the confinement and reformation of male persons, convicted of felonies, who have not been before convicted of crime punishable by imprisonment in a state prison, and who are, at the time of their conviction, between the ages of sixteen and thirty years.

[New.]

§ 7. State prisons.—State prisons are for the imprisonment of persons over the age of sixteen years convicted of felonies and sentenced thereto for terms of one year or more.

[New.]

§ 8. Warden.—The agent and warden of a state prison is designated in this chapter as the warden thereof.

[New. By article V, § 4, of the constitution, the term "agent and warden" is used. For convenience of reference and use in this chapter, such officer is to be designated as the warden.]

§ 9. Superintendent.—The term "superintendent" when used in this chapter, unless otherwise indicated, means the superintendent of state prisons.

[New.]

§ 10. Commission.—The term "commission" when used in this chapter, means the state commission of prisons.

[New.]

§ 11. Prisoner.—The term "prisoner" as used in this chapter means a person imprisoned in a penal institution, or detained therein or held in custody elsewhere, under process of law, or arrest.

[New.]

§ 12. Political division.—The term "political division," when used in this chapter, includes a county, city, village, town or school district.

[New.]

ARTICLE II.

JAILS.

Section 20. Maintenance of jails.

21. Supervision, management and control.

22. Removal of prisoners from one jail to another in same county.

23. Number of rooms.

24. Separation of prisoners.

25. Custody of prisoners.

26. Conversations of prisoners.

27. Food of prisoners.

28. Reading matter; divine service.

29. Jail physician.

30. Prisoner committed for contempt.

Section 31. Commitments by United States courts.
 32. Record of commitments.
 33. Keepers to present list of prisoners detained, to courts.
 34. Prisoners to be discharged if not indicted.
 35. Removal of prisoners by writ of habeas corpus.
 36. Prisoner to be discharged if unable to pay fine.
 37. Sheriff or other officer not to receive anything of value from a prisoner.
 38. Charges for jail accommodations.
 39. Service of papers on prisoner.
 40. Conveyance of prisoners through other counties.
 41. Removal of prisoners in case of fire.
 42. Removal of sick or injured prisoners.
 43. Designation of another place as county jail.
 44. Copy of designation to be served on sheriff of contiguous county.
 45. When and how designation to be revoked.
 46. Houses of detention for witnesses.
 47. Jail, prisoners and papers to be delivered to new sheriff.
 48. Statement of delivery.
 49. Orders of arrest to be delivered to and returned by new sheriff.
 50. Delivery, how enforced.

[General note.—We have included in this article a revision of the present statutes relating to the maintenance, management and control of jails; the custody, treatment and separation of prisoners therein; the designation of the jail of another county as the jail of a county whose jail has been destroyed or abandoned, and all other matters pertaining to jails and the confinement of prisoners therein.

As will be observed by the notes to the several sections, the article is derived from §§ 94-103 of the county law (L. 1892, chap. 686) and the several sections of the code of civil procedure relating to jails and jail discipline. There seems no good reason why provisions concerning the management of a jail should be retained in the code of civil procedure, which should properly be restricted to matters of practice in civil courts. The transfer of the sections of the county law above referred to, is made so that this chapter may contain all substantive law relating to jails.]

§ 20. Maintenance of jails.—There shall be in each county one or more jails. The maintenance of such jails and the inmates thereof shall be a county charge.

[By the County L., § 230, sub. 7, it is provided that "the expenses necessarily incurred in the support of persons charged with, or convicted of crimes, and committed to the jails of the county," are a charge upon the county.]

§ 21. Supervision, management and control.—The sheriff of each county shall have the general supervision, management and control of the jails thereof, and the custody of the persons confined therein; and such jails shall be kept by him, or by keepers appointed by him, for whose acts he shall be responsible. The term "keeper," when used in this article, means the sheriff or the person appointed by him to keep the jail.

[County L., § 183, provides that: "Each sheriff shall have the custody of the jails of his county, and the prisoners therein and such jails shall be kept by him, or by keepers appointed by him, for whose acts he shall be responsible." The first sentence of the proposed section is a re-enactment of the substance of such section of the county law. A similar provision is also found in § 121 of the code of civil procedure. The last sentence of the proposed section is new.]

§ 22. **Removal of prisoners from one jail to another in same county.**—The sheriff of a county having more than one jail may confine a person committed thereto in either, and may remove him from one jail to another, whenever, for any reason, he deems it necessary.

[This section is derived from § 122 of the code of civil procedure. The changes made are verbal.

The section of the code reads as follows:

" The sheriff of a county in which there is more than one jail, may confine a prisoner in either, and may remove him from one jail to another, within the county, whenever he deems it necessary for his safe keeping or for his appearance at court."]

§ 23. **Number of rooms.**—Each jail shall contain a sufficient number of rooms:

1. For the separate confinement of persons detained as witnesses in criminal cases, or committed on civil process or for contempt.

2. For the separate confinement of persons awaiting the action of a grand jury or trial after indictment.

3. For the solitary and separate confinement of prisoners under sentence, while such prisoners are not employed as provided by this chapter.

[County L., § 91. The proposed section does not modify the present law, except that the words " while such prisoners are not employed as provided by this chapter " are added in subdivision 3. It is proposed that persons detained as witnesses be confined apart from those charged with crime. Such persons should in no case be classed as criminals. We have deemed it more appropriate to class such persons with civil prisoners.]

§ 24. Separation of prisoners.—All persons confined in jail shall, as far as practicable, be kept separate from each other. In no case shall a prisoner, arrested in a civil cause, or detained as a witness or for contempt, be kept in the same room or allowed to associate with a prisoner convicted of crime, or detained on a criminal charge; nor shall a person in confinement awaiting the action of a grand jury, or trial after indictment, be kept in the same room or allowed to associate with a prisoner convicted of crime.

Female prisoners shall not be kept in the same room or allowed to associate with male prisoners. But a husband and his wife may be kept together in a room wherein there are no other prisoners.

[County L., § 92, in part, and code of civil procedure, §§ 123, 124. The parts of § 92 of the County Law not contained in this section, will be found in §§ 25, 26, post.

We have inserted the words " or allowed to associate with."

As the law now reads a woman "detained in jail upon a criminal charge, or as a convict under sentence, shall not be kept in the same room with a man; and if detained on civil process, or for contempt, or as a witness, she shall not be put or kept in the same room with a man, except with her husband, in a room in which there are no other prisoners." The language is modified by the revision, but with no material change. Section 124 of the code of civil procedure is the same as the part of § 92 of the County Law which is quoted.]

§ 25. Custody of prisoners.—Each sheriff shall receive and safely keep in the jails of his county, all persons lawfully committed to his custody, for safe-keeping, examination or trial, or sentenced to imprisonment therein upon conviction of a contempt or criminal offense. He shall not, without lawful authority, let any such person out of jail.

[This section is a proposed re-enactment of the first two sentences of § 92 of the County Law.]

§ 26. Conversations of prisoners.—All persons confined in a jail shall be allowed to converse with their counsel, or religious adviser, under such reasonable regulations and restrictions as the keeper of the jail may prescribe. Prisoners under sentence shall not be allowed to converse with any other person, except in the presence of a keeper. The keeper may prevent all other conversation by prisoners when he shall deem it necessary or proper.

[County L., § 92, the last three sentences, with no change.]

§ 27. Food of prisoners.— All persons committed to a jail, except civil prisoners supporting themselves, shall be provided with a sufficient quantity of plain but wholesome food at the expense of the county; but all prisoners, except those under sentence, may, at their own expense and under the direction of the keeper, be supplied with any other proper articles of food.

[This section is derived from the first sentence of § 93 of the County Law, as amended by L. 1896, chap. 826. By such section, it is provided that "prisoners detained for trial and those under sentence shall be supported at a county expense." The language of the proposed section recognizes the charge imposed upon the county for the support of civil prisoners, when they declare, under oath, that they are unable to support themselves, as provided in § 113 of the code of civil procedure.]

§ 28. Reading matter; divine services.— The keeper of a jail shall provide a Bible to be kept in each room thereof. He shall permit the persons therein confined to be supplied with other suitable and proper books and papers. He shall cause divine services to be conducted for the benefit of the prisoners, at least once each Sunday, if there is a room in the jail that may be safely used for that purpose. All prisoners may attend such services.

[County L., § 94. Under the present law it is provided that the sheriff shall cause divine services to be held in the jail, if practicable, and if there is a room in the jail that may be safely used for that purpose. The words "if practicable" are omitted in the revision. It is proposed that divine services shall be held if there is a suitable room in the jail.]

§ 29. Jail physician.— The board of supervisors of each county, except the counties entirely embraced within the city of New York. must appoint some reputable physician, duly authorized to practice medicine, as the physician to the jail of the county. If there is more than one jail, they must appoint a physician to each. The sheriff of each county embraced entirely within the city of New York must appoint a similar physician to each jail within such county. The physician to a jail holds his office at the pleasure of the board or officer who appointed him, except in the county of Kings. In that county, the term of his office is three years.

[Code Civ. Pro., § 126. The section of the code now provides that in the city of New York, the common council appoint a physician to the jail of that city and county. Since the passage of the Greater New York charter, the city embraces all of the counties of New York, Kings and Richmond, and it is therefore proposed to authorize the sheriff of each county in such city to appoint the jail physician to each jail under his charge.]

§ 30. Prisoner committed for contempt.— A prisoner committed to jail upon process for contempt or for misconduct in a case prescribed by law, must be actually confined and detained within the jail, until he is discharged by due course of law or is removed to another jail or place of confinement in a case prescribed by law. A sheriff or keeper of a jail, who suffers such a prisoner to go or be at large out of his jail, except by virtue of a writ of habeas corpus, or by the special direction of the court committing him, or in a case specially prescribed by law, is liable to the party aggrieved for his damages sustained thereby and is guilty of a misdemeanor. If the commitment was for the nonpayment of a sum of money, the amount thereof with interest is the measure of damages.

[Code of Civ. Pro., § 157, with no change.]

§ 31. Commitments by United States courts.—A keeper of a jail shall receive and keep therein every person duly committed thereto charged with or convicted of an offense against the United States, if sentenced to imprisonment for less than one year, by any court or officer of the United States within this state, until he shall be duly discharged, and such person so committed shall be supported therein at the expense of the United States.

[County L., § 96. The words "charged with or convicted of" are inserted for the word "for." The words "if sentenced to imprisonment for less than one year" are new. The same reason exists for prohibiting the imprisonment of United States criminals convicted of felony in county jails as in penitentiaries. It is contrary to the present policy of our penal institutions to authorize imprisonment of convicted criminals of the grade of felons, in county jails.]

§ 32. Record of commitments.— Each keeper shall keep a record of the date of entrance, name, cause of commitment, by whom committed, age, sex, color, place of residence when committed, and date and manner of discharge of each person delivered to his charge. In the case of a prisoner received under a sentence, such record shall also contain the offense for which he was sentenced, term of sentence, fine imposed, if any, place of birth, social relations, education, religious belief, trade or occupation, how employed, when arrested and number of previous convictions.

[The first sentence of this section is new. The second sentence is derived from County Law, § 95. Under the proposed section the same records of prisoners received under sentence will be required as under the present law. The only change in the section is to require a different record of prisoners not detained under sentence.]

§ 33. Keepers to present list of prisoners detained, to courts.— Each keeper shall present to every term of the supreme and county courts having a grand jury, to be held in his county, at the opening of the court, a list stating:

1. The name of every prisoner then detained in such jail other than those under sentence, and United States prisoners.

2. The time when he was committed and by virtue of what precept.

3. The cause of his detention.

[County L., § 97. The word "list" is used instead of "calendar." The present law requires the sheriff to present the names of all prisoners detained in jail. We have excepted prisoners under sentence and United States prisoners. The evident intention of the present law is to inform the courts having grand juries of the names and characteristics of prisoners detained awaiting the action of such courts.]

§ 34. Prisoners to be discharged if not indicted.—Within twenty-four hours after the discharge of a grand jury the court shall cause every person confined in a jail on a criminal charge to await the action of the grand jury, who has not been indicted, to be discharged without bail, unless satisfactory cause shall be shown for his further detention, or, if the case may require, on bail, until the meeting of the next grand jury in the county.

[County L., § 98, without change.]

§ 35. Removal of prisoner by writ of habeas corpus.—During a term of the supreme court having a grand jury in any county, no person detained in a jail of such county upon a criminal charge, shall be removed therefrom by writ of habeas corpus, unless such writ shall have been issued by or shall be made returnable before such court.

[County L., § 99, without change.]

§ 36. Prisoner to be discharged if unable to pay fine.—The county court may, in its discretion, discharge a person confined in a jail of such county for the nonpayment of a fine, not exceeding two hundred and fifty dollars, imposed for a criminal offense and against whom no other cause of detention exists, on satisfactory proof being made to the court that he is and has been ever since his conviction unable to pay such fine.

[County L., § 100. See Code of Crim. Pro., § 484, relating to the power of a court to remit a fine.]

§ 37. Sheriff or other officer not to receive anything of value from a prisoner.—A sheriff or other officer shall not charge, demand or receive from a person whom he has arrested or has in control, any money or other valuable thing for anything furnished or provided for the officer or for the prisoner at any hotel, saloon or other place; nor shall he demand or receive from such prisoner, while in his custody, a gratuity or reward, upon any pretense, for keeping him out of jail, for going with him or waiting for him to find bail, or to agree with his adversary, or for any other purpose.

[The first clause of this section is derived from § 113 of the Code of Civ. Pro. The present law prohibits a charge for " any drink, victuals or other thing furnished or provided for the officer or for the prisoner at any tavern, ale-house, or public victualing or drinking house." No change in substance is made by the revision.

The last clause is now § 114 of the Code of Civ. Pro., and is inserted without change.]

§ 38. **Charges for jail accommodations.**—A sheriff, jailor, or other officer shall not demand or receive money or any valuable thing for chamber rent in a jail, or any fee, compensation, or reward for the commitment, detaining in custody, release, or discharge of a prisoner, other than the fees expressly allowed therefor by law.

[Code Civ. Pro., § 117, without change.]

§ 39. **Service of papers on prisoner.**—A sheriff or jailor, upon whom a paper in an action or special proceeding, directed to a prisoner in his custody, is lawfully served, or to whom such a paper is delivered for a prisoner, must, within two days thereafter, deliver the same to the prisoner, with a note thereon of the time of the service thereof upon, or the receipt thereof by him. For a neglect or violation of this section, the sheriff or jailor guilty thereof is liable to the prisoner for all damages occasioned thereby.

Subject to reasonable regulations prescribed by the sheriff, access to a prisoner shall be allowed for the personal service, when necessary, of a paper in an action or special proceeding to which the prisoner is a party.

[Code Civ. Pro., §§ 131, 132, without change.]

§ 40. Conveyance of persons through other counties.—A sheriff or other officer who has lawfully arrested a prisoner, may convey him through one or more counties, in the ordinary route of travel, from the place where the prisoner was arrested, to the place where he is to be delivered or confined.

A prisoner so conveyed, or the officer having him in custody, is not liable to arrest in any civil action or special proceeding, while passing through another county.

[Code Civ. Pro., §§ 118, 119, without change.]

§ 41. Removal of prisoners in case of fire.—If a jail or a building near a jail is on fire, and there is danger that the prisoners confined in the jail may be injured or may escape, the sheriff or keeper may remove them to some safe and convenient place and there confine them until they can be safely returned to the jail, or, if the jail is destroyed or unfit or unsafe for the confinement of the prisoners, until a place is designated as prescribed in this chapter; and when so designated the prisoners may be removed thereto, and confined therein.

[Code Civ. Pro., § 143, without change.]

§ 42. Removal of sick or injured prisoners.—If the physician or acting physician of a jail and the keeper thereof certify in writing that a prisoner confined therein is sick or injured, and that treatment or a surgical operation is required, which can not be furnished or performed within the jail, the county judge, or in the county of New York, one of the justices of the supreme court of the first judicial district, may, upon application by any person, order the removal of such prisoner to a proper hospital designated by such judge or justice, nearest to such jail. If such prisoner is confined in such jail awaiting trial or the action of a grand jury, notice of the time and place of making such application shall be given to the district attorney of the county wherein such prisoner is to be tried.

The chief officer of the hospital to which such prisoner is removed shall have the custody of and detain such prisoner until he is sufficiently recovered to be returned to the jail. Upon notice of such recovery, the keeper of the jail shall resume the custody of his prisoner.

[There is at present no provision authorizing the removal of a prisoner confined in a jail for medical or surgical treatment, except in case of a civil prisoner. The effect of the proposed section is to extend the power of removal of prisoners for treatment to all prisoners. Some change has been made in the revision. We insert § 127 of the code of civil procedure for comparison:

§ 127. Removal of sick prisoners.—If the physician to a jail, or, in case of a vacancy, a physician acting as such, and the warden or jailor, certify in writing, that a prisoner, confined in the jail in a civil cause, is in such a state of bodily health, that his life will be endangered, unless he is removed to a hospital for treatment, the county judge, or, in the city and county of New York, one of the justices of the supreme court, must, upon application, make an order, directing the removal of the prisoner to a hospital within the county, designated by the judge; or, if there is none, to such nearest hospital as the judge directs; that the prisoner be kept in the custody of the chief officer of the hospital, until he has sufficiently recovered from his illness, to be safely returned to the jail; that the chief officer of the hospital then notify the warden or jailor, and that the latter thereupon resume custody of the prisoner. If the prisoner actually escapes, while going to, remaining at, or returning from the hospital, a new execution may be issued against his person, if he was in custody by virtue of an execution; or, if he was in custody by virtue of an order of arrest a new order of arrest may be granted, upon proof by affidavit of the facts specified in this section, without other proof, and without an undertaking.]

§ 43. Designation of another place as county jail.—Whenever:

1. There is no jail in the county; or

2. The jail becomes unfit or unsafe for the confinement of some or all of the prisoners; or

3. The jail is destroyed by fire or otherwise; or

4. A pestilential disease breaks out in the jail or in its vicinity, and the jail physician certifies that it is likely to endanger the health of any or all of the prisoners therein;

The county judge or, in the county of New York, the presiding justice of the appellate division of the supreme court of the first department, shall designate, by an instrument in writing filed with the county clerk, a suitable place within the county or the county jail of a contiguous county for the confinement of some or all of the prisoners. The place so designated thereupon becomes, except as otherwise prescribed by law, the jail of the county for which it was designated, for the purposes specified in such instrument. Such designation may be modified by the judge or justice making the same, by a like instrument filed with the county clerk.

[Code Civ. Pro., § 135, without change, except that the cases when another jail may be designated are placed in subdivisions. The last sentence is taken from Code Civ. Pro., § 136.]

§ 44. **Copy of designation to be served on the sheriff of contiguous county.**—The county clerk must serve a copy of the designation, duly certified by him under his official seal, on the sheriff and keeper of the jail of a contiguous county so designated. The sheriff of that county must receive into his jail and there safely keep all persons who may be lawfully confined therein, and who are delivered to him by the sheriff of the county for which the designation is made. He is responsible for their safekeeping, as if he was the sheriff of the county for which the designation is made.

[Code Civ. Pro., § 137, without change.]

§ 45. **When and how designation to be revoked.**—When the reason for the designation of another jail or place has ceased to exist, the designation must be revoked by the same authority and in the same manner as it was made, and the revocation shall be filed in the office of the clerk of the county for which such designation was made.

The county clerk must immediately serve a copy of the revocation, duly certified by him under his official seal, upon the sheriff of the same county; who must remove the prisoners belonging to his custody, and confined without his county or in any other place, to the proper jail of such county.

[Code Civ. Pro., §§ 136, 141, 142, first sentence.

Section 141 of the code provides that "When a jail is erected for the county, for whose use the designation was made, or its jail is rendered fit and safe for the confinement of prisoners, or the reason for the designation of another jail or place has otherwise ceased to be operative, the designation must be revoked, as prescribed in this article." Section 136 of the code prescribes that "The designation may be modified or revoked, by the judge making the same, by a like instrument in writing, filed with the clerk of the county." It will thus be seen, by a comparison, that the revision contemplates no change in the substance of the law.

The last paragraph of the proposed section is the same as the first sentence of § 142 of the code.]

§ 46. Houses of detention for witnesses.—The board of supervisors of any county may provide for the erection, lease or purchase of a suitable building or place separate and distinct from the jail of the county, for the safekeeping and care of all persons detained as witnesses, or confined under civil process or committed for a contempt, to be termed a house of detention. When such a building or place is provided, the sheriff of the county shall confine therein all such persons. The sheriff shall have the same charge and control of such house and shall be entitled to the same compensation for the care and keeping of prisoners therein, as in the county jail. Upon the application of the district attorney of such county, the county judge may order the removal of any person so confined to the county jail.

[Section 101 of the County Law authorizes the lease or purchase of a suitable place for the detention of women and children charged with "crime not punishable by death or imprisonment in state prison for a term exceeding five years or with second offense, and persons detained as witnesses, to be termed houses of detention; and when so provided, any magistrate in the county shall commit women and girls, and boys under sixteen years, and all persons held as witnesses thereto, instead of the jail." It will be noticed that by the proposed section, houses of detention are only to be used for the confinement of civil prisoners and witnesses. All persons charged with crime should be committed to jail, there to be separated and dealt with as the law and the sound discretion of the sheriff demands; but it is proper, if houses of detention are erected, that civil prisoners should be confined therein, without association with criminals.]

§ 47. Jail prisoners and papers to be delivered to new sheriff.—Where a new sheriff has been elected or appointed, and has qualified and given the security required by law, the clerk of the county must furnish to the new sheriff a certificate under his hand and official seal, stating that the person so appointed or elected, has so qualified and given security. After the term of office of a new sheriff begins and within ten days after he has filed his oath of office and undertaking as required by law, and served the county clerk's certificate to that effect upon the former sheriff, or other officer lawfully executing the office of sheriff, such former sheriff or other officer shall deliver to the new sheriff:

1. The jails of the county, all the property of the county pertaining thereto, and all the prisoners confined therein.

2. All process, orders, commitments and other papers and documents authorizing or relating to the confinement or custody of a prisoner, or, if such a process, order or commitment has been returned, a statement, in writing, of the contents thereof and when and where it was returned.

[Code Civ. Pro., §§ 182, 183, 184, subs. 1-3. Section 182 is to be re-enacted without change. Section 183 is omitted, as it is unnecessary. Section 184, subs. 1-3, are contained in the proposed section without change, except that former subs. 1 and 2 are consolidated.]

§ 48. Statement of delivery.—At the time of such delivery the former sheriff, or other officer executing the office of sheriff, shall make a written statement in duplicate, specifying:

1. The property, documents and prisoners delivered.

2. The process or other authority by which each prisoner was committed and is detained, and whether the same has been returned or is delivered to the new sheriff.

Both statements shall be delivered to the new sheriff, one of which shall be filed in his office and the other returned to the former sheriff, or other officer or person making such delivery, with an acknowledgment indorsed thereon of the receipt of the property, documents and prisoners specified therein.

[Code Civ. Pro., § 185. The present law requires the former sheriff to execute an instrument stating the facts as specified in the proposed section. Such instrument is to be delivered to the new sheriff, who "must acknowledge, in writing, upon a duplicate thereof, the receipt of the property, documents and prisoners therein specified; and deliver such duplicate and acknowledgment to the former sheriff." It will be noticed that the statement to be required by the revision is to be made in duplicate, one of which is to be indorsed by the new sheriff and returned to the former sheriff. This is a simpler and more convenient procedure.]

§ 49. *Orders of arrest to be delivered to and returned by new sheriff.*—Where a person, arrested by virtue of an order of arrest, is confined, either in jail or within the liberties thereof, at the time of assigning and delivering the jail to the new sheriff, the order, if it is not then returnable, must be delivered to the new sheriff and be returned by him at the return day thereof, with the proceedings of the former sheriff and of the new sheriff thereon.

[Code Civ. Pro., § 187, without change.]

§ 50. **Delivery, how enforced.**—If the former sheriff, or other officer executing the office of sheriff, neglects or refuses to deliver to the new sheriff, the jail or any of the property, documents or prisoners in his charge, such new sheriff shall, notwithstanding, take possession of the jail, and of the property of the county therein, and the custody of the prisoners therein confined, and proceed as prescribed by law to compel the delivery of the documents withheld.

[Code Civ. Pro., § 188. The words " or other officers executing the office of sheriff " are new, and are inserted to reach the case of a coroner who is acting as sheriff.]

ARTICLE III.

CONFINEMENT OF CIVIL PRISONERS; JAIL LIBERTIES.

Section 60. Definition of civil prisoner.

 61. Confinement and support of civil prisoners.

 62. Board and supplies furnished to civil prisoners confined outside of a jail.

 63. Term of imprisonment of civil prisoners.

 64. Confinement of civil prisoners in New York city.

 65. Prisoners under United States process.

 66. Indictment of civil prisoners.

 67. Existing jail liberties.

 68. Alteration and establishment of jail liberties.

 69. Resolution establishing or altering jail liberties to be filed and posted.

 70. Effect of designation of another place or jail upon jail liberties.

Section 71. Who entitled to jail liberties; undertaking.

72. Justification of sureties.

73. Civil prisoner to be committed when surety is insufficient.

74. Surrender of civil prisoner by his sureties.

75. What constitutes an escape.

76. Liability for escape.

77. Action against either the sheriff or the sureties for an escape.

78. Stay of proceedings upon judgment when action is brought against sheriff.

79. Voluntary return or recapture a defense.

80. Effect of judgment in an action against the sheriff.

81. Judgment for sheriff in action against sureties.

82. Stay of judgment for sheriff against sureties.

83. Judgment against sheriff is evidence of damages.

84. Duties of coroner, when sheriff is a party to an action or special proceeding.

85. Arrest of sheriff by coroner.

86. Confinement of sheriff by coroner; jail liberties.

87. Duties of coroner when sheriff is plaintiff.

88. Civil prisoner in custody of coroner entitled to jail liberties, etc.; escape.

[General note.—The sections of the code of civil procedure, (§§ 110-119, 145-189) relating to the confinement, treatment and maintenance of civil prisoners in jails; the establishment of jail liberties and the right thereto of such prisoners, and the liability for the escape of a civil prisoner are included in this article, without material change. An attempt has been made to harmonize and simplify the present law. Many superfluous and useless provisions have been omitted. The object and result of the present law are retained.]

§ 60. Definition of civil prisoner.—The term "civil prisoner," as used in this article, includes a person arrested and confined by virtue of an execution issued upon a judgment rendered in a civil court, or of an order of arrest in an action or special proceeding in such court, or surrendered in exoneration of his bail in such an action or proceeding.

[We have defined the term "civil prisoner" for convenience of use in this article. Section 110 of the code of civil procedure prescribes the persons who shall be confined by virtue of a civil mandate. By the proposed section the term "civil prisoner" is made to include all of these.]

§ 61. Confinement and support of civil prisoners.—A civil prisoner shall be safely kept in custody in the manner herein prescribed, until he satisfies the judgment rendered against him or is discharged according to law. He shall be supported at his own expense, unless he makes oath before the sheriff that he is unable to support himself during his imprisonment, in which case he shall be supported in the jail at the expense of the county.

[Code Civ. Pro., §§ 110, 112. Section 110 is included in this section without change except that the word "civil prisoner" is used, instead of all that it implies as provided in the foregoing section. Section 112 is revised but no change is made in effect. It is proposed, as now, that if the prisoner swears that he is unable to support himself, "his support shall be a county charge." It is proposed by the revision that if a civil prisoner is supported at a county expense that "he shall be supported in the jail." This provision is new.]

§ 62. Board and supplies furnished to civil prisoner confined outside of a jail.—The officer arresting or the person having the custody of a civil prisoner and keeping him at a place other than the county jail shall not demand or receive a greater sum for lodging, drink, food or any other thing, than the rate prescribed by the county court, or, if no rate has been prescribed, than the sum allowed by a justice of the peace of the town or city where the prisoner is kept, upon proof that such lodging, drink, food or other thing was actually furnished to the prisoner at his request. Such officer or person shall not demand or receive any compensation for strong, spirituous or fermented liquor or wine, sold or delivered to the prisoner.

A civil prisoner kept at a place other than the county jail may purchase or procure such food, drink, bedding, linen and other necessary things as he may desire, from whomsoever he pleases. Such person or officer shall not detain any part of such articles, or demand or receive any pay therefor.

[Code of Civ. Pro., §§ 115, 116.
Section 115 provides that "if a person arrested is kept in a house other than the jail of the county, the officer arresting him, or the person in whose custody he is, shall not demand or receive from him any greater sum, for lodging," etc. It will be noticed that the proposed section is made to apply to a civil prisoner kept at "a place other than the county jail." It is evident from the context, that the section of the code revised was intended to apply only to civil prisoners.

Section 116 is contained in the last paragraph of the proposed section, with no change except that the present law specifies more in detail the articles which a civil prisoner may procure.]

§ 63. Term of imprisonment of civil prisoners.—No person shall be imprisoned within the prison walls of a jail for a longer period than three months under an execution or any other mandate against the person to enforce the recovery of a sum of money less than five hundred dollars in amount, or under a commitment upon a fine for contempt of court in the non-payment of alimony or counsel fees in a divorce case, where the amount so to be paid is less than the sum of five hundred dollars; and where the amount in either of said cases is five hundred dollars or over, such imprisonment shall not continue for a longer period than six months. All such prisoners in the custody of the sheriff shall be discharged at the expiration of such periods without formal application therefor. No person shall be imprisoned within the jail liberties of a jail for a longer period than six months upon any execution or other mandate against the person, and no action shall be commenced against the sheriff or upon a bond given for the jail liberties by such person to secure the benefit of such liberties, for an escape made after the expiration of such six months imprisonment.

[Code Civ. Pro. § 111, all except last two sentences, without change.]

§ 64. Confinement of civil prisoners in New York city.—The places in the city of New York designated for the confinement of prisoners in civil causes, shall be the jails of the counties in which they are situated for the confinement of such prisoners. The sheriffs of the counties of New York, Kings and Richmond, shall have the custody of such jails situated in their respective counties, and of the prisoners therein.

[Code Civ. Pro., § 120, with such changes as are made necessary by the incorporation of the counties of Kings and Richmond, in the city of New York.]

§ 65. Prisoners under United States process.—A sheriff must receive and keep in the jails of his county, prisoners committed thereto by virtue of civil process issued by a court of record of the United States until they are discharged by the due course of the laws of the United States, in the same manner as if they were committed by virtue of mandates in civil actions issued from courts of this state. The sheriff may receive, to his own use, the money payable by the United States for such use of the jail, unless otherwise provided by law.

A sheriff or jailor, to whose jail civil prisoners are lawfully committed by the courts of the United States, is answerable for their safe keeping, in the courts of the United States, according to the laws thereof.

[Code Civ. Pro., §§ 133, 134, without change, except that the words "unless otherwise provided by law," at the end of the first paragraph, are new. They are inserted in view of provisions contained in acts making the office of sheriff a salaried office in certain counties.]

§ 66. Indictment of civil prisoners.—Where a civil prisoner has been indicted for a criminal offense, the court in which the indictment is pending may make an order, requiring the sheriff in whose custody he is, to bring him before the court; whereupon the court may make such disposition of the prisoner as to it seems proper. The sheriff's fees and expenses, in so doing, are a charge on the county wherein the court is sitting.

[Code Civ. Pro., § 156, without change.]

§ 67. Existing jail liberties.—The liberties of the jail for each of the following counties shall be:

1. For the county of New York, the whole of that county.

2. For the county of Onondaga, the whole of the city of Syracuse.

3. For the county of Monroe, the whole of the city of Rochester.

4. For the county of Erie, the whole of the city of Buffalo.

5. For the county of Dutchess, the whole of the city of Poughkeepsie.

6. For the county of Kings, the whole of that county.

7. For the county of Richmond, the whole of that county.

8. For the county of Albany, the whole of the city of Albany.

9. For the county of Jefferson, the whole of the city of Watertown.

10. For the county of Herkimer, the whole of the village of Herkimer.

11. For the county of Rensselaer, the whole of the city of Troy.

12. For the county of Niagara, the whole of the city of Lockport.

The liberties of the jail in each of the other counties of the state, as they now exist, shall continue to be the liberties thereof, until they are altered, or new liberties are established.

[Code Civ. Pro., §§ 145, 146, without change, except that sub. 7, prescribing the jail limits of the county of Richmond, is inserted. This change is made because of including Richmond county in the city of New York, and the abolition of the board of supervisors of Richmond county. Under such circumstances it is better that the jail limits in such county should be fixed by statute.]

§ 68. Alteration and establishment of jail liberties.—In all counties, except those named in the last preceding section, the liberties of a jail may be altered or established by resolution of the board of supervisors, approved by the county judge. Such liberties shall contain a space of ground, adjacent to the jail not exceeding five hundred acres in extent, laid out as nearly as may be in a rectangle or square. A stream of water, canal, street or highway may be adopted as an exterior line notwithstanding it is not in a straight line or is not at right angles with the other exterior lines of the jail liberties. A resolution establishing or altering jail liberties must contain a particular description of their boundaries, and immediately after its adoption such boundaries must be designated by monuments, inclosures, posts or other visible and permanent marks, at the expense of the county.

[Code Civ. Pro., § 147.

The power to establish and alter the boundaries of jail liberties was vested in the board of supervisors by L. 1857, ch. 482, § 1, sub. 18. This act was repealed by the county law (L. 1892, chap. 686), but sub. 18 was not re-enacted. We have in this section reinvested the board of supervisors with power to establish or alter such boundaries.

By § 147 of the code it is provided that "as soon as may be" after the adoption of the resolution the boundaries shall be designated by monuments, etc. In the last sentence of the proposed section such designation is to be made "immediately."]

§ 69. Resolution establishing or altering jail liberties.—The resolution establishing or altering jail liberties shall be filed in the office of the county clerk immediately upon its adoption. The county clerk must, within one week after the filing of such resolution, deliver an exemplified copy thereof to the keeper of the jail who must keep the same exposed to public view, in an open and public part of the jail, and exhibit it to each person admitted to the liberties of the jail, at the time of his executing a bond for that purpose.

[Code Civ. Pro., § 148. The first sentence is new in terms, although the present law contemplates the filing of the resolution in the office of the county clerk. Otherwise there is no change proposed by the revision.]

§ 70. Effect of designation of another place or jail upon jail liberties.—If the jail of a contiguous county, or any other place, is designated as the county jail of a county, pursuant to this chapter, after a civil prisoner has been admitted to the liberties of the jail of the county for which such designation is made, or if, after such designation and before he is removed, he becomes entitled to such liberties, such prisoner shall, notwithstanding such designation, remain within the liberties of the jail to which he was committed. But the sheriff may remove such prisoner to the jail or other place so designated, and confine him therein, if he might confine him in the jail of his own county.

If a prisoner confined in or removed to the jail of a contiguous county, becomes entitled to the liberties of the jail, the sheriff of that county must admit him to the jail liberties of that county as if he had been originally arrested by that sheriff on a mandate directed to him.

[Code Civ. Pro., §§ 138, 139, 140.

Sections 138 and 139 are consolidated and included in the first paragraph of the proposed section. The two sections of the code prescribe two cases where a civil prisoner is entitled to the jail liberties of the county where he was committed, notwithstanding the designation of the jail of another county as the jail of that county. By the consolidation it is unnecessary to repeat the parts of such sections which are identical.

The last paragraph is a proposed re-enactment of § 140 of the code without change.]

§ 71. Who entitled to jail liberties; undertaking.—A civil prisoner in the custody of a sheriff is entitled to the liberties of the jail upon delivering to the sheriff an undertaking conditioned that the person so in custody will remain a prisoner and will not escape or go without the liberties of the jail until legally discharged.

Such undertaking must be executed by the prisoner and one or more sufficient sureties, residents and householders or freeholders of the county, or by any fidelity or surety company authorized by law to transact business in this state. The penalty of each undertaking shall be as follows:

1. If the prisoner is in custody under an order of arrest, or has been surrendered in exoneration of his bail, before judgment, twice the sum in which the sheriff was required to hold him to bail.

2. If he is in custody under an execution, twice the sum directed to be collected by the execution.

3. If he has been surrendered after judgment, twice the amount remaining uncollected upon a judgment against him.

Such undertaking shall be held for the indemnity of the sheriff taking it, and of the party at whose instance the prisoner executing it, is confined.

[Code of Civ. Pro., § 149, part of §§ 150 and 151.

Section 149 provides that "a person in the custody of the sheriff, by virtue of an order of arrest; or of an execution in a civil action; or in consequence of a surrender in exoneration of his bail; is entitled to be admitted to the liberties of the jail," etc. Such a person is a civil prisoner under the definition contained in § 60 of the revision, ante.

The condition of the undertaking is the same as that in § 150 of the code. There is no change in the method of executing such undertaking, except that the revision expressly authorizes the execution by a fidelity or surety company.

It is necessary to insert this provision, as by making such section of the code a part of this chapter, § 811 of the code, authorizing the execution of bonds and undertakings by surety companies, would not be applicable.

The penalties of undertakings for jail liberties contained in the proposed section are the same as those contained in § 150 of the code. The last paragraph is a proposed re-enactment of § 151 of the code without change.]

§ 72. Justification of sureties.—The provisions of the code of civil procedure relating to the justification of bail, the notice of justification of the sureties, the officers before whom they must justify, the substitution of new sureties or a new undertaking, the examination and qualifications of the new sureties and the allowance of the undertaking, as contained in chapter seven, title one, article three of such code, are applicable to the undertaking required to secure the benefit of jail liberties, unless it is otherwise expressly prescribed in this article.

[Code Civ. Pro., § 150, in part.

This section is a re-enactment of the last sentence of such § 150 without change.]

§ 73. Civil prisoner to be committed when surety is insufficient.—If the party at whose instance the civil prisoner is in custody discovers that a surety upon the undertaking is insufficient, he may, upon proof of the fact by affidavit or otherwise, apply to the court, or a judge thereof, on whose process or mandate such prisoner is in custody, or to the county judge of the county where such prisoner is confined, and the court or a judge thereof or such county judge may make an order committing such prisoner to close confinement in the jail until another undertaking with good and sufficient sureties is offered.

[Code Civ. Pro., § 152. without change.]

§ 74. Surrender of civil prisoner by his sureties.—One or more of the sureties in an undertaking given for the liberties of the jail, may surrender the principal at any time before judgment is rendered against them in an action on the undertaking; but they are not exonerated thereby from a liability incurred before making the surrender.

The surety or sureties making such surrender must take the principal to the keeper of the jail, who shall, upon his or other written requisition to that effect, take the principal into his custody, indorse upon the undertaking given for the liberties an acknowledgment of the surrender, and, if required, give the sureties a certificate, acknowledging the surrender.

[Code Civ. Pro., §§ 153, 154, without change.]

§ 75. What constitutes an escape.—The going at large beyond the jail liberties, by a civil prisoner, without the assent of the party at whose instance he is in custody, is an escape, and the sheriff in whose custody he was, or the sureties on his undertaking, may pursue and retake him, as if he had escaped from the jail.

[Code Civ. Pro., § 155, in part.

That part of such of the code which determines what constitutes an escape is contained in the proposed section. The part of such section which prescribes what is not an escape is omitted as unnecessary. The liability for an escape is contained in the next section of the revision.]

§ 76. **Liability for escape.**—Before an undertaking for the liberties of the jail is delivered to the sheriff, the sheriff is alone liable in an action against him for the escape of a civil prisoner. After the delivery of such an undertaking and before its acceptance or approval as provided by law, the sheriff and the sureties on the undertaking are liable for such escape in an action brought against any or all of them.

After the acceptance or approval of such undertaking the sureties thereon are alone liable in an action against them for such escape.

The extent of such liability is as follows:

1. The damages sustained by the judgment creditor, if the prisoner was in custody by virtue of an order of arrest, or in consequence of a surrender in exoneration of his bail before judgment.

2. The amount of debt, damages or sum of money for which the prisoner is committed, if he was in custody by virtue of any other mandate, or in consequence of a surrender in exoneration of his bail after judgment.

The voluntary return of a prisoner to the liberties of the jail from which he escaped, or his recapture by or surrender to the sheriff from whose custody he escaped, before the commencement of an action for an escape, is a good defense therein. In an action against the sureties on an undertaking, the defendants may make any defense thereto, which might be made by the sheriff in an action against him for an escape.

[Code Civ. Pro., §§ 158, 160.

By § 158 of the code the liability of the sheriff for an escape of a civil prisoner is not terminated "until an undertaking for the liberties of the jail is given and approved."

The present law recognizes the liability of sureties on the undertaking after its delivery and before its approval. Section 149 of the code provides that the prisoner shall be admitted to jail liberties upon delivery of the undertaking. From the time of the delivery of the undertaking to the time of its approval, the sheriff and the sureties are jointly liable for an escape.

In the revision we have declared specifically the liabilities incurred by the sheriff and the sureties. No change is made in substance. The only effect is to clearly determine the several liabilities.

The last paragraph is derived from § 160 of the code.]

§ 77. Action against either the sheriff or the sureties for an escape.—If a civil prisoner escapes after an undertaking for the liabilities of the jail is delivered to the sheriff and before it is accepted or approved as provided by law, the party at whose instance the prisoner was confined, or, in case of his death, his executor or administrator, may elect to bring an action against the sheriff or the sureties on the undertaking. The commencement of an action against the sureties on the undertaking shall be deemed an election, and bars an action against the sheriff or other officer accepting such undertaking, on account of the escape of the prisoner executing the undertaking, unless such escape was with the assent of the sheriff or other officer.

[Code Civ. Pro., §§ 166, 167, 168.

By § 166 it is provided: "If an undertaking for the jail liberties is forfeited before the same is duly allowed the party at whose instance the prisoner was confined, or, in case of his death, his executor or administrator, may elect to bring an action on the undertaking." This section authorizes an action for an escape against either the sheriff or the sureties on an undertaking, if the escape occurs after the delivery of the undertaking and before its approval. No change in result is made by the revision.

Section 167 is omitted. In view of imposing the liability upon the sureties, by the preceding section, it is not necessary to say that an action for an escape may be maintained against the sureties.

The last sentence is a proposed re-enactment of § 168, without change.]

§ 78. Stay of proceedings upon judgment, when action is brought against sheriff.—If the party at whose instance the civil prisoner was confined, or his executor or administrator, elects to bring an action against the sheriff for the escape, the court may, except where the escape was made with the sheriff's assent, stay proceedings upon a judgment recovered against the sheriff, with such limitations, and upon such terms as it deems just, until he has had a reasonable time to prosecute the undertaking, and collect a judgment recovered thereon.

[Code Civ. Pro., § 170, without change, except that the words "party at whose instance the civil prisoner was confined, or his executor or administrator, elects to" are inserted in place of the words "person so entitled to bring an action on the undertaking for the jail liberties in lieu of making such election."]

§ 79. Voluntary return or recapture a defense.—In an action against a sheriff or other officer, for the escape of a prisoner, it is a defense, that the escape was without the assent of the defendant, and that at the commencement of the action, he had the prisoner within the liberties, either by his voluntary return, or by recapture.

[Code Civ. Pro., § 171, without change.]

§ 80. Effect of judgment in an action against the sheriff.—If, in an action brought against the sheriff for the escape of a civil prisoner after the delivery of an undertaking, and before its acceptance or approval, due notice of the pendency of the action was given the prisoner and his sureties, to enable them to defend the same, and a judgment has been rendered against the sheriff, such judgment is conclusive evidence of the right of the sheriff to recover against the prisoner and his sureties, to whom the notice was given, as to any matter which was or might have been controverted in the action against the sheriff.

[Code Civ. Pro., § 161.
The words "after the delivery of an undertaking and before its acceptance or approval" are new. No change in result is thus effected, as under the present law the sheriff is not liable for an escape after the approval of the undertaking. The clause is inserted for the sake of clearness.]

§ 81. Judgment for sheriff in action against sureties.—In an action brought by the sheriff against the sureties on an undertaking, the court must order a summary judgment for the plaintiff, upon motion made in behalf of the sheriff, if it appears that judgment has been rendered in an action against him for the escape of the prisoner, and that due notice of the pendency of such action was given to the prisoner and his sureties, to enable them to defend the same.

Such judgment must thereupon be entered, with costs.

To entitle a sheriff to move for such a judgment a copy of his complaint must have been served upon the prisoner and his sureties, and at least twenty days notice of the motion be given to them.

[Code Civ. Pro., §§ 162, 163, without change.]

§ 82. Stay of judgment for sheriff against sureties.—If it appears, upon the hearing of the motion, that the defendants have a meritorious defense, which was not and could not have been controverted in the action against the sheriff, the court may stay proceedings on the judgment, with such limitations and upon such terms, as it deems just, until a trial in the action.

But the judgment must stand as security for the sheriff. If the defense is established, the court must vacate the judgment, and render judgment for the defendant.

[Code Civ. Pro., § 164, without change.]

§ 83. Judgment against sheriff is evidence of damages.—In an action brought by a sheriff against the sureties on an undertaking for the jail liberties, a judgment against him for the escape of the prisoner, is evidence of the damages sustained by him, as if it had been collected; and he may recover his reasonable attorney's and counsel fees, and other expenses in defending the action against him, as part of his damages.

[Code Civ. Pro., § 165, without change.]

§ 84. Duties of coroner, when the sheriff is a party to an action or special proceeding.—In an action or special proceeding, to which the sheriff of a county is a party, a coroner of the same county has all the power, and is subject to all the duties of a sheriff, in a cause to which the sheriff is not a party, except as otherwise specially prescribed by law.

A mandate in a civil action or special proceeding which must or may be executed by the coroners, or by a coroner of a county, must be directed either to a particular coroner, or generally to the coroners of that county. Where such a mandate is directed generally to the coroners of a county, or requires them to do any act, it may be executed, and a return thereto may be made and signed, by one of them; but such an act or return does not affect the others.

[Code Civ. Pro., §§ 172, 173, without change.]

§ 85. Arrest of sheriff by coroner.—Where a mandate requiring the arrest of the sheriff of a county is directed to a coroner, he must execute the same in the manner prescribed by law for the execution of a similar mandate by a sheriff; and he may take an undertaking on the arrest, or an undertaking for the jail liberties, in a like case and manner, and with like effect, as where such an undertaking is taken by a sheriff.

[Code Civ. Pro., § 174, without change.]

§ 86. Confinement of sheriff by coroner; jail liberties.—Where the actual confinement of a sheriff by a coroner, on a mandate, is required or authorized by law, he must be confined by the coroner, in a house situated within the liberties of the jail of the county, other than the sheriff's house or the jail, in the same manner as a sheriff is required by law to confine a prisoner in the jail. Such house thereupon becomes the jail of the county, for the use of the coroner; and each provision of law relating to the jail, or to an escape from the jail, applies thereto, while the sheriff is confined therein.

A sheriff so arrested must be admitted to the liberties of the jail of the county, in a like case, and upon executing a like undertaking to the coroner, as prescribed by law for a prisoner in the sheriff's custody.

If the sheriff escapes, the coroner and the sureties on such undertaking are liable in the same manner and to the same extent, and are entitled to the same defenses, as in the case of the escape of a civil prisoner from a sheriff. All the provisions of this article relating to actions for an escape are applicable to an escape of a sheriff when confined as a civil prisoner.

[Code Civ. Pro., §§ 175, 176, 177, 178.
The first three sections are included without change. Section 178 is not re-enacted word for word. It is deemed sufficient to cover the provisions thereof by a reference to other similar provisions in this article.]

§ 87. Duties of coroner when sheriff is plaintiff.—A person arrested by a coroner, in an action or special proceeding, in which the sheriff of the county is plaintiff, must be confined in the jail of the county, in a case where such a confinement is required, or authorized by law; but the coroner is not liable for an escape of the prisoner from the jail, after he has been confined therein. A person so confined must be kept and treated, in all respects, like a prisoner confined by the sheriff.

[Code Civ. Pro., § 179, without change.]

§ 88. Civil prisoner in custody of coroner entitled to jail liberties, et cetera; escape.—A person so arrested by a coroner, is entitled to be discharged, or to the liberties of the jail, in the same case and in like manner, and under the same conditions as a civil prisoner in the custody of the sheriff. The undertaking given for the jail liberties by a person so arrested must be similar in all respects to that required to be given to a sheriff; and it has the like effect and may be proceeded upon in the same manner.

A coroner is answerable for an escape of a civil prisoner, admitted by him to the liberties of the jail, in the same manner and to the same extent as a sheriff, and may interpose a like defense.

[Code Civ. Pro., §§ 180, 181. The first sentence of § 180 reads as follows: "A person so arrested by a coroner, is entitled to be discharged, or to the liberties of the jail, as the case requires, upon giving an undertaking to the coroner, in the like manner, and in a like case, in which a person arrested by a sheriff would be entitled to be discharged, or to the liberties." The change proposed in the language by the revision does not alter the meaning.

The remaining parts of the two sections referred to are revised without change.]

ARTICLE IV.

PENITENTIARIES.

Section 90. Establishment of penitentiaries.

91. Officers and employes not to be interested in purchases.

92. County contracts with penitentiaries.

93. Convicts sentenced to penitentiaries for felonies.

94. Payments to discharged prisoners sentenced for felonies.

95. Imprisonment of tramps.

96. Auditing of penitentiary accounts against the state.

§ 90. Establishment of penitentiaries.—The penitentiaries heretofore established are continued, and shall be managed and controlled as provided by the several acts relating thereto.

The board of supervisors of any county may establish and maintain a penitentiary for the confinement of persons convicted of misdemeanors within such county and subject to the provisions of this chapter, provide for the imprisonment and employment of all persons sentenced thereto.

[The first sentence is new. The remainder is derived from § 102 of the County Law, which authorizes a board of supervisors to establish and maintain a county work-house.]

§ 91. Officers and employes not to be interested in purchases.—No manager, superintendent, officer or employe of a penitentiary shall be interested directly or indirectly in the furnishing of materials, labor or supplies for the use of the penitentiary, or in any contract made or entered into for the benefit or in behalf of such penitentiary.

[This section is new.]

§ 92. County contracts with penitentiaries.—The board of supervisors of a county may contract with the board of supervisors of any county having a penitentiary or with the board, committee, commissioner or officer, having charge of such penitentiary, for the confinement and maintenance in such penitentiary of any person who may be sentenced thereto for a term of sixty days or more, by any court or magistrate in such county.

A notice of the making of such contract and of the period of its continuance shall be published once in each week for at least four consecutive weeks in at least two newspapers published in the county making such contract, and also in the county where such penitentiary is situated.

[L. 1859, chap. 289, § 1, as amended by L. 1874, chap. '209.

The present law provides that "It shall be lawful for the several boards of supervisors in the several counties of this state to enter into an agreement with the boards of supervisors of any county having a penitentiary therein, or with any in their behalf by them appointed to receive and keep in the said penitentiary any person or persons who may be sentenced to confinement therein by any court or magistrate, in any of the several counties in this state, for any term not less than sixty days."

The last paragraph of the proposed section is a revision of the last sentence of § 1 of L. 1859, chap. 289.

The changes made are verbal.]

§ 93. Convicts sentenced to penitentiaries for terms of one year or less.—The superintendent or other officer having charge of a penitentiary shall not receive a convict sentenced thereto for a single offense for a term of more than one year, nor any person convicted of felony, (except a male convict between the ages of sixteen and twenty-one years, sentenced for less than one year.)

All prisoners in a penitentiary, when this chapter takes effect, sentenced thereto by the courts of this state for an offense punishable by imprisonment in a state prison, shall continue to be maintained therein at the expense of the state until the expiration of their respective terms. The state shall pay for the maintenance of all prisoners sentenced thereto for a felony the sum of thirty cents per day.

[New.

By the Penal Code, § 699, as amended by L. 1896, chap. 553, and §§ 703, 704, it is evident that no person can now be sentenced to a penitentiary unless the term of imprisonment is fixed at less than one year. The amendment made to § 699 by L. 1896, chap. 553, was probably intended to supersede § 1 of L. 1875, chap. 571, as amended by L. 1895, chap. 372, and L. 1875, chap. 529.

We have attempted to make clear in this section the evident intent of the legislature to provide for the maintenance of all state convicts in state prisons. It is desirable that misdemeanants be separated from felons; to bring this about we have provided in effect that no person shall be sentenced to a penitentiary for a term of more than one year.]

§ 94. Payments to discharged prisoners sentenced for felonies.—The superintendent of each penitentiary shall furnish to each prisoner sentenced thereto prior to the passage of this chapter, for a term of more than one year, for an offense punishable by imprisonment in a state prison, upon his discharge therefrom, by pardon or otherwise, necessary clothing not exceeding twelve dollars in value, except for the time between the first day of November and the first day of April, when clothing not exceeding eighteen dollars in value may be given. He shall also pay to such prisoner the sum of five dollars, and the further sum of four cents for each mile to be necessarily traveled by such prisoner in traveling by the shortest route from the penitentiary to his place of residence, if within the state, and if not, to the place of his conviction. The amount expended by the penitentiary in carrying out the provisions of this section shall be a charge upon the state.

[L. 1879, chap. 471, § 1.

The words "prior to the passage of this chapter" are new. As the law now is, no prisoners can be confined in penitentiaries and maintained at a state expense. The proposed section only applies to prisoners sentenced to penitentiaries before the passage of L. 1896, chap. 553.]

§ 95. Imprisonment of tramps.—All tramps sentenced to a penitentiary as prescribed by the penal code shall be supported and maintained therein at the expense of the state at a rate of thirty cents per day per capita.

[L. 1885, chap. 490, § 1, provides that the expense of the imprisonment of tramps shall be a charge against the state, at the rate of thirty cents per day per capita.]

§ 96. Auditing of penitentiary accounts against the state.— The superintendent of each penitentiary shall annually on the thirteenth day of September return to the state comptroller a detailed statement showing the amount due such penitentiary for the maintenance of prisoners sentenced thereto for offenses punishable by imprisonment in a state prison, for expenditures for clothing, payments to and transportation of discharged prisoners and for the support and maintenance of tramps sentenced thereto as provided by law. Such statement shall be verified by the oath of the superintendent and set forth:

1. The name of each prisoner sentenced thereto for offenses punishable by imprisonment in a state prison, the offense of which he was convicted, the date of his conviction, the term for which he was sentenced and date of his reception in the penitentiary.

2. The name of each prisoner discharged with the date of such discharge and the facts in relation to such prisoner required by the preceding subdivision.

3. The name of each tramp for the support of whom the state is chargeable, with the name of the committing magistrate, the

date and place of his commitment, and the date of his reception in the penitentiary and the date of his discharge.

The comptroller shall audit and allow the amount found to be due such penitentiary under the provisions of this article, and draw his warrant therefor on the state treasurer in favor of the superintendent of such penitentiary, payable from any money in the state treasury appropriated for that purpose.

[This section retains the present method of auditing penitentiary accounts against the state. The sections of the present statutes relating to the payment of charges against the state for the maintenance of prisoners in penitentiaries, etc., are consolidated without material change. See L. 1875, chap. 571, § 3, as amended by L. 1895, chap. 372, and L. 1879, chap. 471, §§ 2 and 3.]

ARTICLE V.

REFORMATORIES.

Section 100. Location and names of state reformatories.

    101. Board of managers.

    102. General powers and duties of managers.

    103. Appointment and removal of officers and employes.

    104. Compensation of officers and employes.

    105. Oaths and bonds.

    106. General duties of superintendent.

    107. General duties of chaplain.

    108. General duties of physician.

    109. Powers and duties of treasurer.

    110. Monthly estimates of expenses; contingent fund.

    111. Monthly statements of receipts and expenditures.

    112. Affidavit of superintendent; vouchers.

    113. Purchases.

Section 114. Transportation of convicts to reformatories.

 115. Transfer of prisoners to state prisons.

 116. Transfers from state prisons to reformatories.

 117. Transfer from one reformatory to another.

 118. Control and discipline of prisoners.

 119. Register of prisoners.

 120. Parole of prisoners.

 121. Retaking of paroled prisoners.

 122. Rules and regulations.

 123. Marks for good conduct; records filed with secretary of state.

 124. Absolute release from imprisonment.

 125. Sentences for a definite period.

 126. Supervision of paroled prisoners.

 127. Reports to governor.

[General note.—This article is applicable to the Elmira Reformatory and the Eastern Reformatory at Napanoch, Ulster county, now in course of construction. We have included chapter 711 of the Laws of 1887, relating to the Elmira Reformatory, and made it applicable to the Eastern Reformatory, when ready for occupancy.

We have specified in detail the powers and duties of the superintendent, chaplain, physician and treasurer. The requirements of monthly estimates, statements of receipts and expenditures, purchases of supplies, and vouchers, are new in form although similar requirements are contained in the annual appropriation act of each year.

It is also provided that prisoners transferred to a state prison shall be received therein as prisoners under an indeterminate sentence, and may therefore be released on parole or absolutely discharged by the board of parole of the prison. Under the present law provision is made for a transfer to a state prison, but no way is provided for the release or discharge of a prisoner so transferred until the expiration of the maximum term "provided by law for the crime for which the prisoner was convicted and sentenced," unless the board of managers require his return.

Cases have arisen which seem to show injustice and hardship to a transferred prisoner because of this system. Transferred prisoners are seldom, if ever, recalled to the reformatory. The result follows that a prisoner sentenced by a judge to a reformatory, under the impression that a light punishment is being imposed, is made to suffer much more severely than was intended.

By the proposed law, the prisoner immediately upon his transfer to a state prison is subject to the exclusive control of the prison officers and the jurisdiction of the managers of the reformatory ceases. He becomes entitled to all the privileges of a prisoner under an indeterminate sentence. He may be paroled by the board of parole and his maximum sentence may be commuted for good conduct. Other changes proposed by this article are noted at the end of the several sections.]

§ 100. Location and names of state reformatories.—The state reformatory at Elmira is continued and shall be known as the Elmira reformatory.

The state reformatory at Napanoch, Ulster county, shall, when completed, be known as the Eastern reformatory. The provisions of this article shall apply alike to both reformatories, except as otherwise provided.

[New.]

§ 101. Board of managers.— Each reformatory shall be under the management of a board of five managers, who shall be appointed by the governor by and with the advice and consent of the senate. The full term of office of each manager shall be five years. The managers of the Elmira reformatory in office when this chapter takes effect, shall be continued in office until the expiration of their respective terms. The managers of the Eastern reformatory shall be appointed when such reformatory is completed and ready for occupancy. Such appointment shall take effect immediately and shall be for terms of one, two, three, four and five years, respectively, from the first day of January succeeding the time of making such appointments. Their successors shall thereafter be appointed for a term of five years.

When the term of office of a manager of the Elmira reformatory expires at a time other than the last day of December, the term of office of his successor is abridged so as to expire on the last day of December, preceding the time when such term would otherwise expire, and the term of office of each manager of such reformatory thereafter appointed shall begin on the first day of January.

The managers of each reformatory may organize as a board by electing from their number a president, a secretary and a treasurer. The treasurer shall be the treasurer of the reformatory. Such managers shall receive no compensation for their services but shall be allowed their reasonable traveling and other official expenses.

[L. 1887, chap. 711, § 1.

The present board of managers of the Elmira reformatory is to be continued in office without change of term. It is proposed that the Eastern reformatory be managed by a board of like number, appointed in the same manner and for the same term. The terms of office of the managers are in each instance to begin on the first day of January. To accomplish this purpose, the second paragraph, relating to the abridgement of the terms of the successors of the managers of the Elmira reformatory now in office, is inserted. This change is proposed to conform with the provisions in other general laws for the commencement of the terms of officers appointed by the governor upon the first day of

January. Under the present law the terms of the managers of the Elmira reformatory begin on the first day of May.

The words "and when the senate is not in session, by the governor, subject to the consent and approval of the senate when it shall convene," found in § 1 of L. 1887, chap. 711, are omitted. The provisions of the general law relating to appointment by the governor and senate should be made applicable to managers of the reformatory. See Public Officers L., §§ 7, 28, as amended by L. 1898, chap. 655. The sentence, "Whenever a vacancy shall occur in such board by the refusal of either of the members thereof to act or otherwise, such vacancy, for the unexpired term thereof, shall be filled in like manner." is also omitted. Public Officers L., § 28, is to a similar effect and should be applied to such managers.

The sentence: "The governor may remove any of the managers for misconduct, incompetency, or neglect of duty after opportunity shall be given them to be heard, upon written charges." which is at the end of such § 1. is also omitted. Public Officers L., §§ 23, 24, relate to removals by the governor and are applicable to boards of managers of reformatories.

The sentence in the proposed section relating to the organization of the board is new.]

§ 102. General powers and duties of managers.— The board of managers of each reformatory shall:

1. Have the general superintendence, management and control of such reformatory, of the grounds and buildings, officers and employes thereof, of the prisoners therein, and of all matters relating to the government, discipline, contracts and fiscal concerns thereof.

2. Make rules and regulations, not inconsistent with law for the proper government of such reformatory and of the officers and employes thereof, and for the employment, discipline, education, transfer, parole and discharge of prisoners sentenced thereto.

3. Investigate the affairs of such reformatory, inquire into any

improper conduct alleged to have been committed by any officer or employe, and require reports from the superintendent and other officers thereof in relation to the discipline, labor and government of such reformatory and have power to take proof under oath in any such investigation or inquiry.

4. Meet at least once in each month at the reformatory for the purpose of performing the several duties prescribed in this article.

5. Examine, monthly or quarterly, all the accounts, expenditures and vouchers relating to the business of such reformatory, and certify their approval or disapproval thereof to the comptroller.

6. Report to the legislature, annually, on or before the tenth day of January, for the year ending with the last day of the next preceding September, the condition of such reformatory, the amount of money received and expended by them during such year with a detailed statement thereof; their proceedings in regard to the prisoners therein, and such other matters as they may deem proper, or as the legislature may require.

7. Make such other reports from time to time as the legislature may require.

[L. 1887, chap. 711, §§ 2, 10, 11.

Subdivision 1 is a re-enactment of the first clause of the first sentence of such section, which provides that such "board of managers shall have the charge and general superintendence of the grounds and buildings for said reformatory;" the rest of such sub. 1 is new.

Subdivision 2 is new. But by § 11 of the act of 1887, the board of managers is authorized to "establish rules and regulations under which prisoners within the reformatory may be allowed to go upon parole outside of the reformatory buildings;" and in the same section the board is authorized "to make all rules and regulations necessary and proper for the employment, discipline, instruction, education, removal and temporary or conditional release and return, as aforesaid, of all convicts in said reformatory." By § 10 of such act the board of managers is required to provide for reformatory discipline, which necessarily implies the power to make rules and regulations relating thereto.

Again, in § 13, it is made the duty of the managers "to maintain such control over all prisoners committed to their custody, as shall prevent them from committing crime, best secure their self-support and accomplish their reformation." It is evident, then, that although no general power to make rules and regulations is expressed in the present law, special powers are imposed upon the board, in such a manner as to render it necessary for them to make such rules and regulations.

Subdivisions 3 and 4 of the proposed section are new.

Subdivision 5 of such section is a re-enactment of the second sentence of L. 1887, chap. 711, § 2, without change.

Subdivision 6 is a re-enactment of the last sentence of § 2 of the present law.

Subdivision 7 is new.]

§ 103. Appointment and removal of officers and employes.— The board of managers of each reformatory may appoint a general superintendent, one or more chaplains and a physician, and remove either of them for good and sufficient cause, upon written charges preferred after an opportunity to be heard.

The superintendent of each reformatory may appoint and remove at pleasure other officers, guards, keepers and employes, the number of which shall be determined by the board of managers. Such superintendent shall also appoint, by and with the advice and consent of the board of managers, such foremen and instructors as may be necessary, any of whom may be removed by the board of managers or by the superintendent.

[L. 1887, chap. 711, §§ 3, 4.

The present law makes it the duty of the superintendent to appoint the chaplains and physician. Such officers should be appointed by the boards of managers and be responsible to them. We have proposed that the office of financial agent be abolished. The financial affairs of the reformatory are under the direct control of the superintendent. Under the existing circumstances the office is useless. We do not, therefore, propose a re-enactment of any part of § 4 of the former act.

For the sake of comparison we insert that part of the present § 3 relating to the subjects embraced in the proposed section:

"The said board of managers shall appoint a general superintendent of said reformatory, and shall have power to remove him for cause, after opportunity shall be given him to be heard upon written charges. The said general superintendent shall, by and with the advice and consent of the board of managers, appoint such foremen and instructors as may be necessary, any of whom may be removed by the board of managers or by the general superintendent. All other officers, guards and employes at said reformatory, except the financial agent, shall be appointed by the general superintendent and be removable at his pleasure."

Under the present law no provision is made for the appointment of a chaplain.

It is suggested that the office of chaplain is as important in a reformatory as a state prison. The utility of the office is generally recognized, and there seems no valid reason why such an officer should not be connected with our state reformatories.]

§ 104. Compensation of officers and employes.— The annual compensation of the several officers, guards and keepers of each reformatory shall be fixed by the board of managers, but shall not exceed the following sums: To the superintendent, the sum of three thousand and five hundred dollars; to the physician, one thousand five hundred dollars; to the clerk, one thousand dollars; to the principal keeper, one thousand dollars; to the chaplain or chaplains, one thousand dollars; to the kitchen keeper, eight hundred dollars; to the storekeeper, eight hundred dollars; to the hall-keeper, six hundred dollars; to the yardkeeper, six hundred dollars; to the keepers, each, six hundred dollars; to the guards, each, five hundred dollars. Maintenance and supplies may be allowed to such officers in the discretion of the board of managers.

[L. 1887, chap. 711, § 5.
The salaries of the several officers are not changed. No reference is made to the salary of the financial agent, since it is proposed to abolish that office. The provision for the chaplain or chaplains is new.

The clause at the end of § 5 of the act of 1887, which reads as follows, is omitted: " And if, for any reason, the term of service of any of them shall terminate before the end of any year, their compensation shall be paid only for the term of service, at the rate of the annual compensation above provided, and such salaries shall be in full for all services performed by them." This clause seems unnecessary.]

§ 105. Oaths and bonds.—All persons appointed to office as prescribed in this article shall take the constitutional oath of office and file the same in the office of the secretary of state within fifteen days after such appointment. The superintendent and such other officers and employes, as may be so required by the comptroller, shall give bonds to the state in such sums and with such sureties as he shall approve, conditioned for the faithful performance of their lawful duties.

[L. 1887, chap. 711, § 6, without change.]

§ 106. General duties of superintendent.—The superintendent of each reformatory, subject to the direction and control of the board of managers, shall:

1. Have the general supervision and control of the reformatory, of the grounds and buildings, subordinate officers and employes thereof, the prisoners therein, and of all matters relating to the government and discipline thereof.

2. Make such rules, regulations and orders, not inconsistent

with law, or with the rules, regulations and directions of the board of managers, as he may deem proper or necessary for the government of such reformatory and of the officers and employes thereof; and for the employment, discipline and education of the prisoners sentenced thereto.

3. Annually report to the board of managers, on or before the first day of December, all such matters as are required by the board of managers.

4. Exercise such other powers and perform such other duties as the board of managers may lawfully prescribe.

[New. Section 3 of L. 1887, chap. 711, last sentence, reads as follows: " The remaining duties of the general superintendent shall be such as may be prescribed by the board of managers, and except as in this act otherwise provided, the general superintendent shall be subject to the control and direction of the board of managers."

The proposed section (sub. 4), authorizes the board of managers to prescribe other powers and duties of the superintendent.]

§ 107. General duties of chaplain.—The chaplain or chaplains of each reformatory shall:

1. Hold religious services in the reformatory, under such rules and regulations as the board of managers may prescribe, and attend to the spiritual wants of the prisoners.

2. Personally communicate with each prisoner at least once in each week, for the purpose of giving them religious and moral instruction, under such regulations as the board of managers may prescribe.

3. Visit daily the sick in the hospital.

4. Perform such other duties, consistent with his calling and profession, as the board of managers may direct.

[New. The present law does not recognize, in any way, the office of chaplain. See note to § 103, ante.]

§ 108. General duties of physician.—The physician of each reformatory shall:

1. Have charge of the hospital of the reformatory, under the direction of the board of managers, and keep a daily record of all admissions thereto, in such form as the board of managers may prescribe.

2. Attend to the medical needs and prescribe the diet of the sick prisoners in the hospital or cells.

3. Examine daily, and as often as required by the superintendent, all prisoners undergoing punishment by solitary confinement or otherwise, and prescribe the allowance of food to each prisoner so confined.

4. Make such reports to the board of managers, as to the sanitary condition of the reformatory and the general health of the prisoners, as he may see fit, and such other reports as may be required by the board of managers, the superintendent or the state commission of prisons.

5. Hold himself in readiness at all times to discharge his duties as such physician, whenever directed by the superintendent.

6. Perform such other duties as may be prescribed by the rules and regulations of the board of managers.

[New. While the present law recognizes the office of physician, his duties are not specified.

The duties of this important officer should not be left solely to the will of the general superintendent or the board of managers.]

§ 109. Powers and duties of treasurer.—The treasurer of each reformatory shall:

1. Have the custody of all moneys received from the comptroller on accounts of estimates made by the superintendent and revised and approved by the comptroller and keep an accurate account thereof.

2. Collect and receive all moneys due the reformatory from any source.

3. Deposit all such money in a bank designated by the comptroller, conveniently near the reformatory, in his name as treasurer, and send each month to the comptroller a statement showing the amount so received and deposited, and from whom and for what received, and when such deposits were made. Such statement of deposits shall be certified by the proper officer of the bank receiving such deposit. The treasurer shall attach to such statement an affidavit to the effect that the sum so deposited is all the money received by him from any source, since making the last statement. A bank designated by the comptroller to receive such deposits shall, before any deposit is made, execute a bond to the people of the state, in a sum and with sureties approved by the comptroller, conditioned for the safe-keeping of the funds deposited.

4. Pay out money deposited for the uses of the reformatory, upon the vouchers of the superintendent, in accordance with the estimates made by the superintendent and revised and approved by the comptroller.

5. Cause to be kept full and accurate accounts of all receipts and expenditures in the manner and form prescribed by the comptroller.

[New. The present law contains no regulation of the powers and duties of the treasurer.

The act of 1887 does not attempt to regulate the finances of Elmira reformatory. It is proposed that the treasurer perform duties similar to those of such officers in other state institutions.]

§ 110. Monthly estimates of expenses; contingent fund.— The superintendent of each reformatory shall, on or before the fifteenth day of each month, cause to be prepared duplicate estimates in minute detail, of the expenses required for the reformatory under his charge for the ensuing month. He shall countersign and submit one of such duplicates to the comptroller, and retain the other to be placed on file in the office of the reformatory. The comptroller may cause such estimates to be revised either as to quantity or quality of supplies and the estimated cost thereof. Upon the revision and approval of such estimates, the comptroller shall authorize the board of managers of such reformatory to make drafts on him, as the money may be required for the purposes mentioned in such estimates, which drafts shall be paid on his warrant, out of the funds in the treasury of the state appropriated for the support of such reformatory. In every such estimate there shall be a sum named, not to exceed two hundred and fifty dollars, as a contingent fund, for which no minute detailed statement need be made. No expenditure shall be made from such contingent fund, except in case of actual emergency, requiring immediate action, and which cannot be deferred without loss or danger to the reformatory, or the inmates thereof. No payments shall be made on account of goods furnished, salaries of officers, or wages of employes, unless they are contained in the estimate provided in this section, and duly approved by the comptroller.

[This section is new. But in the general appropriation law of 1897, monthly estimates were required of each reformatory. The adoption of this and the following section will not materially modify the present financial system of the reformatory.]

§ 111. Monthly statements of receipts and expenditures.—The treasurer of each reformatory shall, on or before the fifteenth day of each month, make to the comptroller, a full and perfect statement of all the receipts and expenditures, specifying the several items, for the last preceding calendar month. Such statement shall be verified by the affidavit of the treasurer attached thereto, in the following form:

I .... treasurer of the .... do solemnly swear that I have deposited in the bank designated by law for such purpose all the moneys received by me on account of such .... during the last month; and I do further swear that the foregoing is a true abstract of all the moneys received, and expenditures made by me or under my direction as such treasurer during the month ending on the .... day of 18   .

[New. See note to preceding section.]

§ 112. Affidavit of superintendent; vouchers.—There shall be attached to such treasurer's statement, the affidavit of the superintendent, to the effect that the goods and other articles therein specified were purchased and received by him or under his direction at the reformatory, that the goods were purchased at a fair cash market price and paid for in cash, and that neither he nor any person in his behalf had any pecuniary or other interest in the articles purchased; that he received no pecuniary or other benefit therefrom in the way of commission, percentage, deductions or presents, or in any other manner whatever, directly or indirectly; that the articles contained in such bill were received at the institution; that they conformed in all respects to the invoiced goods received and ordered by him, both in quality and quantity. Such statement shall be accompanied by the vouchers, showing the payment of the several items contained in the statement, the amount of such payment and for what the payment was made. Such vouchers shall be examined by the comptroller and compared with the estimates made for the month for which the statement is rendered. If any voucher is found objectionable, the comptroller shall endorse his disapproval thereon, with the reason therefor, and return it to the treasurer, who shall present it to the board of managers for correction and immediately return it to the comptroller. All such vouchers shall be filed in the office of the comptroller.

[This section is new, but conforms with the law relating to the same subject in state prisons.]

§ 113. Purchases.—All purchases for the use of the reformatories shall be made for cash and not on credit or time; every voucher shall be duly filled up at the time it is taken, and with every abstract of vouchers paid there shall be proof on oath that the voucher was filled up and the money paid at the time it was taken. The board of managers shall make all needful rules and regulations to enforce the provisions of this section. No manager, officer or employe of a reformatory shall be interested directly or indirectly, in the furnishing of materials, labor or supplies for the use of such reformatory, nor shall any manager act as attorney or counsel for the board of managers thereof.

[This section is new. But see State Finance Law (L. 1897, chap. 413), §§ 16, 17.]

§ 114. Transportation of convicts to reformatories.—Upon the receipt, by the superintendent of a state reformatory, of notice of the sentence of a convict thereto, an officer of the reformatory shall proceed to the place of conviction, and the sheriff or keeper of the prison having custody of the convict, shall deliver the convict to such officer, with the papers required to be delivered with such convict, and such officer shall thereupon convey such convict to the reformatory at the expense of the reformatory. Such officer shall for the purpose of such conveyance have all the powers possessed by sheriffs in conveying a convict to a state prison in pursuance of law.

[L. 1887, chap. 711, § 8, without change.]

§ 115. Transfer of prisoners to state prisons.—If it shall appear to the board of managers of a reformatory that a prisoner confined therein

1. Was, at the time of his conviction, more than thirty years of age; or

2. Has been previously convicted of a felony; or

3. While in the reformatory, is incorrigible and that his presence therein is seriously detrimental to the welfare of the institution; an application may be made to a justice of the supreme court of the judicial district in which such reformatory is located, for an order transferring such prisoner to a state prison. Such application shall be by written petition signed by the president and secretary of the board and shall state the causes for seeking such transfer and shall have endorsed thereon or attached thereto the consent to such transfer of the superintendent of state prisons, which shall specify the prison to which such prisoner is to be transferred.

Upon proof of the service of such notice, and upon such hearing as the justice may prescribe, such justice shall grant such order of transfer, if it appear to his satisfaction that the facts alleged are true and that such transfer should be made.

A prisoner so transferred shall be confined in such state prison as under an indeterminate sentence, commencing with his imprisonment in the reformatory with a minimum of one year, and a maximum fixed by the court when imposing the sentence, or by statute, if the court has not fixed such maximum; and such prisoner, while in such prison, shall be entitled to commutation of sentence for good conduct, in reduction of said maximum period, as are prisoners sentenced for fixed terms, and may be released on parole or absolutely discharged as are other prisoners confined under an indeterminate sentence, or returned to the reformatory in the discretion of the superintendent of state prisons and with the consent of the board of managers of such reformatory.

[By L. 1887, chap. 711, § 11, first sentence, it is provided that: "The board of managers shall have power to transfer temporarily with the written consent of the superintendent of prisons, to either of the state prisons, or in case any prisoner shall become insane, to the state asylum for insane criminals, any prisoner, who, subsequent to his committal, shall be shown to have been, at the time of his conviction more than thirty years of age, or to have been previously convicted of crime, and may also so transfer any apparently incorrigible prisoner whose presence in the reformatory appears to be seriously detrimental to the well being of the institution. And such managers may, by written requisition, require the return to the reformatory of any person who may have been so transferred."

It is proposed by the revision that an order of the court be secured before any transfer be made to a state prison. A prisoner transferred to a state prison is to remain at such prison until the expiration of "the maximum term provided by law for the crime for which the prisoner was convicted and sentenced," unless sooner recalled by the written requisition of the reformatory managers. The board of managers has seldom, if ever, exercised its right of recall. Prisoners sentenced to a reformatory for an offense, the punishment for which should, because of extenuating circumstances, be lenient, can be imprisoned for a much longer term than justice requires. The court often imposes the sentence for the purpose of lessening the rigor of the punishment.

This purpose may be subverted by the board of managers if it appears that the prisoner is more than thirty years of age, has been previously convicted of crime, even of a trivial nature, or while in the reformatory does not conform with the reformatory rules and discipline. The right to transfer to a state prison should be preserved, but it is suggested that the board of managers should not be vested with the power of changing absolutely the form and duration of the imprisonment. We have therefore proposed that the transfer of a prisoner to a state prison be made upon the order of a justice of the supreme court.

The court in sentencing the convict to a reformatory for an indefinite term, recognizes the right of the board of managers to terminate the imprisonment before the expiration of a maximum period. When the prisoner is transferred to a state prison, he is removed from the active surveillance of the reformatory officers, and the determination of the length of his imprisonment should no longer be subject to their control. He is sentenced to imprisonment for an indeterminate term, and that imprisonment, either in the reformatory or a state prison, should be subject to diminution by the good conduct of the prisoner, according to the rules of either institution.

We have therefore provided that when a prisoner is transferred to a state prison he shall be confined therein as under an indeterminate sentence, subject to release at any time prior to the expiration of the "maximum period," by the parole board of the prison.]

§ 116. Transfer from state prisons to reformatories.—Whenever there is unoccupied room in either reformatory, the board of managers thereof may make a requisition upon the superintendent of state prisons, for a sufficient number of well-behaved and most promising convicts under thirty years of age and who are confined in a state prison because of a first offense, and the superintendent of state prisons shall transfer such convicts to such reformatory for education and treatment under the rules and regulations thereof. The board of managers shall receive and detain the prisoners so transferred for the terms of their sentences, if such sentences are for fixed terms, less the commutation of imprisonment that would have been allowed to them for good conduct if they had completed their terms in the state prisons from which they were transferred. If such prisoners are confined under an indeterminate sentence, they may be paroled and discharged as are prisoners confined in a state prison, except that the board of managers shall constitute a board of parole for the purpose of paroling and discharging such prisoners, and such board shall make rules and regulations for such parole and discharge not inconsistent with law and in general conformity with the rules and regulations made by the parole boards of the state prisons.

The provisions of this chapter relating to the terms of commutation of imprisonment for good conduct are applicable to the prisoners so transferred.

[L. 1887, chap. 711, § 12.
The last sentence of the first paragraph is new, and is inserted in view of the fact that prisoners are occasionally sentenced to state prisons for indeterminate sentences, and of the change suggested by this commission as to the imposing of indeterminate sentences in all cases.]

§ 117. **Transfers from one reformatory to another.**—Whenever the Eastern reformatory is completed and ready for occupancy, the state commission of prisons may cause to be transferred thereto from the Elmira reformatory, upon the application of the board of managers of the former and upon due notice to the board of managers of the latter reformatory, as many prisoners as may be deemed practicable, under regulations and in the manner prescribed by such commission.

Prisoners may be transferred from one reformatory to another, after such Eastern reformatory is completed and occupied, whenever the commission may deem it necessary and feasible. No transfer shall be made except upon the application of the board of managers of one reformatory and upon notice of such application to the reformatory from which the transfer is sought to be made.

[This section is new; when the Eastern reformatory at Napanoch is ready for occupancy it will at first be necessary to transfer inmates from Elmira to such reformatory.]

§ 118. Control and discipline of prisoners.—The board of managers of each reformatory shall maintain such control over all prisoners committed to their custody, as shall prevent them from committing crime, best secure their self-support and accomplish their reformation. The discipline to be observed therein shall be reformative and each board of managers may use such means of reformation consistent with the security and improvement of the prisoners, as they may deem expedient. The prisoners therein may be employed in agricultural or mechanical labor as a means of securing their support and reformation.

[The first sentence of this section is a proposed re-enactment of L. 1887, chap. 711, § 13, without change.

The remainder of the section is derived from L. 1887, chap. 711, § 10, without change.]

§ 119. Register of prisoners.— The board of managers of each reformatory shall cause to be entered in a register the date of the admission of each prisoner received therein, the name, age, nativity and nationality of such prisoner, and also such other ascertainable facts relating to parentage and early social influences as seem to indicate the constitutional and acquired defects and tendencies of the prisoner, and based upon these, an estimate of the then present condition of the prisoner and the best probable plan of treatment. There shall also be entered upon such register, quarterly or oftener, minutes of observed improvement or deterioration of character, notes as to methods of treatment employed, all orders or alterations affecting the standing or situation of such prisoner, the circumstances of his final release and any subsequent facts relating to his personal history which may be brought to their knowledge.

[L. 1887, chap. 711, § 13, all except the first sentence, without change.]

§ 120. Parole of prisoners.—The board of managers of each reformatory may allow the prisoners confined therein to go upon parole outside of the reformatory buildings and inclosures. A person so paroled shall remain in the legal custody and under the control of the board until the expiration of the maximum term, or until his absolute discharge as provided by law. No personal appearances before the board shall be permitted in behalf of the parole or discharge of any prisoner.

[L. 1887, chap. 711, § 11.
The words "until the expiration of the maximum term, or until his absolute discharge as provided by law" are new.

The last sentence is a substitute for the sentence: "But no petition or other form of application for the release of any prisoner shall be entertained by the managers."

The power to grant paroles contained in § 11 of the present law is contained in the following sentence thereof: "The said board of managers shall also have power to establish rules and regulations under which prisoners within the reformatory may be allowed to go upon parole outside of the reformatory buildings and inclosure, but to remain, while on parole, in the legal custody and under the control of the board of managers," etc. The power to make rules and regulations is retained in § 122 of the revision.]

§ 121. **Retaking of paroled prisoners.**—If the board of managers of the reformatory from which the prisoner was paroled has reasonable cause to believe that such prisoner has violated the conditions of his parole, the board may issue its warrant certified by its secretary, for the retaking of such prisoner at any time prior to the expiration of the maximum term as provided by law. The time within which the prisoner must be retaken shall be specified in the warrant. Such warrant may be issued to an officer of the reformatory or to any peace officer of the state, who shall execute the same by taking such prisoner into custody within the time specified in the warrant. The officer shall forthwith take such prisoner before the county judge of the county, or a justice of the supreme court of the judicial district in which he is retaken, and such judge or justice upon satisfactory proof that such prisoner has violated his parole, shall by order direct the return of such prisoner to the reformatory from which he was paroled, and thereupon such officer shall return such prisoner to such reformatory, where he may be retained for the remainder of the maximum period of his sentence. The time during which the prisoner was on parole shall not be deemed a part of such maximum term.

[By § 11 of L. 1887, chap. 711, it is provided that the board of managers shall have full power "to retake and reimprison any convict so upon parole, * * * whose written order certified by its secretary, shall be a sufficient warrant for all officers named in it to authorize such officers to return to actual custody any conditionally released or paroled prisoner; and it is hereby made the duty of all officers to execute said order the same as ordinary criminal process."

It will be noticed that under the present law no time is prescribed or required to be specified in the warrant for the retaking of a paroled prisoner. We have inserted the words "at any time prior to the expiration of the maximum term as provided by law."

"The time within which the prisoner must be retaken shall be specified in the warrant." It was not the intention of the present law that a paroled prisoner should be retaken at any time without regard to the expiration of his maximum term. The insertion will make clear the manifest intent of the framers of the original statute.

We have also suggested that the prisoner who has been charged with a violation of the conditions of his parole be given a hearing before a county judge of the county or a justice of the supreme court of the judicial district in which he is retaken. This suggestion should meet with the approval of the legislature, because it is evident that a prisoner on parole should not be deprived of a privilege earned by his good conduct without an opportunity to refute the charges made against him before a tribunal free from all prejudices.]

§ 122. **Rules and regulations.**—The board of managers of each reformatory shall make rules and regulations, not inconsistent with law.

1. Prescribing the conditions under which prisoners may be paroled or conditionally released;

2. Regulating the retaking and reimprisonment of such prisoners;

3. Providing for the employment, discipline, instruction and education of the prisoners.

Such rules and regulations shall be adopted by the resolution of the board of managers passed at a meeting thereof at which a majority of its members shall be present. All rules and regulations heretofore or hereafter adopted and in force shall be printed and a copy thereof distributed to each officer, employe and prisoner in the reformatory.

[L. 1887, chap. 711, § 11, in part.

The last paragraph is new. The following sentences of § 11 of the act of 1887 are revised and included in this section:

"The board of managers shall also have power to establish rules and regulations under which prisoners within the reformatory may be allowed to go upon parole," etc.

"The said board of managers shall also have power to make all rules and regulations necessary and proper for the employment, discipline, instruction, education, removal and temporary or conditional release and return, as aforesaid of all the convicts in said reformatory."]

§ 123. Marks for good conduct; records filed with secretary of state.—The board of managers of each reformatory shall adopt a uniform system of marks by means of which shall be determined the number of marks or credits to be earned by each prisoner sentenced to such reformatory, as the condition of increased privileges, or of release from their control, which system shall be subject to revision from time to time. Each prisoner shall be credited for good personal demeanor, diligence in labor and study, and for results accomplished, and be charged for dereliction, negligence and offences. Each prisoner's account of marks or credits shall be made known to him as often as once a month and oftener if he shall request it. The board of managers shall make rules and regulations by which each prisoner shall be permitted to see and converse with some member of the board of managers at stated periods, without the presence of the superintendent or other officers of the reformatory.

An abstract of the record in the case of each prisoner confined in each reformatory shall be made semi-annually, showing the date of admission, the age, the situation at the time of making such abstract, whether in the reformatory, or state prison, the hospital for insane criminals or elsewhere, whether any and how much progress or improvement has been made, and the reason for release or continued custody or transfer as the case may be. Such abstract shall be considered by the board of managers at a regular meeting and filed with the secretary of state.

[L. 1887, chap. 711, § 14, in part. The part of such section relating to absolute releases is contained in the following section. The sentence relating to applications for release of prisoners is omitted. but see last sentence of § 120 of the revision, which is proposed as a substitute.

The last two sentences of the first paragraph of the above section of the revision are substituted for the following provisions of § 14 of the present law: " The managers shall establish rules and regulations by which the standing of each prisoner's account of marks or credits shall be made known to him as often as once a month, and oftener if he shall at any time request it, and may make provision by which any prisoner may see and converse with some one of said managers during every month."]

§ 124. Absolute release from imprisonment.—When it appears to the board of managers that there is strong or reasonable probability that any prisoner will live and remain at liberty without violating the law, and that his release is not incompatible with the welfare of society, they shall issue to such prisoner an absolute release or discharge from imprisonment. Nothing herein contained shall be construed to impair the power of the governor to grant a pardon or commutation in any case.

[L. 1887, chap. 711, § 14, last and second from the last sentences, without change.]

§ 125. Sentences for a definite period.—If, through oversight or otherwise, a person be sentenced to imprisonment in either of such reformatories for a definite period of time, such sentence shall not, for that reason, be void, but the person so sentenced shall be entitled to the benefits and subject to the liabilities of this article, in the same manner and to the same extent as if such sentence had been made for an indefinite period of time in the manner provided by the penal code.

[L. 1887, chap. 711, § 15. The clause reading "and in such case said managers shall deliver to said offenders a copy of this act, and written information of his relation to said managers" is omitted as unnecessary.]

§ 126. Supervision of paroled prisoners.—The board of managers may appoint and at pleasure remove suitable persons in any part of the state, who shall supervise paroled prisoners and perform such other lawful duties as may be required of them by such board. Such persons shall be subject to the direction of the board. They shall be paid a reasonable compensation for their services and expenses, which shall be a charge upon and paid from the funds of the reformatory.

[L. 1887, chap. 711, § 16, without change.]

§ 127. Reports to governor.—Within ten days after this chapter takes effect, the superintendent of the Elmira reformatory shall report to the governor the names of all prisoners confined therein at the time of making such report, the dates of their sentences and admission to the reformatory, the crime for which they were convicted, the place of their conviction and the court or judge by whom sentenced.

During the first week of each month a similar report shall be made showing similar facts relating to the prisoners admitted to a reformatory, during the preceding month, and containing the names of the prisoners who died, with the causes of their death, and also the names of those who were paroled, absolutely released or transferred, with the name of the institution to which the transfer was made, within such month. The superintendent shall furnish such other information and reports as the governor may require.

[This section is new.]

ARTICLE VI.

STATE PRISONS; OFFICERS.

Section 140. Location and names of state prisons.
141. Superintendent of state prisons; compensation and expenses.
142. Office and clerical force of the superintendent.
143. General powers and duties of superintendent.
144. Annual report of superintendent.
145. Officers and employes.
146. State detective.
147. Qualifications of officers and employes.
148. Compensation of officers of state prisons.
149. Official oaths.
150. Undertakings.
151. General duties of warden.
152. General duties of clerk.

Section 153. General duties of physician.

    154. General duties of chaplain.

    155. General duties of principal keeper.

    156. General duties of store keeper.

    157. General duties of kitchen keeper.

[General note.—This article contains the provisions of the present law relating to the superintendent of state prisons and his general powers and duties; and the appointment, qualifications, compensation and general duties of prison officers. At the end of each section, is a reference to the law from which the section is derived.]

§ 140. Location and names of state prisons.—There shall continue to be maintained for the security and reformation of male convicts in this state, three state prisons; one at Sing Sing, in Westchester county; one at Auburn, in Cayuga county; and one at Dannemora, in Clinton county, which prisons shall respectively be denominated the Sing Sing prison, the Auburn prison and the Clinton prison; and for the security and reformation of female convicts in this state, the state prison for women at Auburn.

[R. S., pt. IV, chap. 3, tit. II, § 29, as amended by
L. 1889, chap. 382.

The word "male" is inserted; the last clause is new. The state prison for women was established by L. 1893, chap. 306, and in that act it was provided that all women convicted of felony were to be sentenced to such prison. See article XII.]

§ 141. Superintendent of state prisons; compensation and expenses.—The superintendent of state prisons shall be appointed in the manner and for the time prescribed by section four of article five of the constitution, and shall perform the duties and possess the powers set forth in such section. He shall be paid an annual salary of six thousand dollars, and all reasonable and necessary expenses incurred by him personally in the discharge of his official duties. He shall file, monthly, with the comptroller an itemized and verified account of his personal and office expenses.

[R. S., pt. IV, chap. 3, tit. II, § 31, as amended by
L. 1889, chap. 382.
Such section reads as follows:

"§ 31. The superintendent of state prisons shall receive an annual salary of six thousand dollars, payable monthly by the treasurer on the warrant of the comptroller, and in addition thereto, all reasonable and necessary traveling expenses by him actually incurred and paid in the discharge of his official duties, not exceeding the sum of five hundred dollars per annum, and a further sum of four thousand nine hundred and fifty dollars per annum, or so much thereof as may be necessary for clerk hire, copying and messenger, postage, stationery and other incidental expenses, of all which expenses he shall keep an account by items and verify the same by his oath to be filed with the comptroller."

The clause fixing the amount to be expended by the superintendent for personal and office expenses is omitted. The legislature each year appropriates for such expenses, without regard to the limitation expressed in this statute.]

§ 142. Office and clerical force of the superintendent.—The superintendent of state prisons shall have his office in the city of Albany. He may appoint a chief clerk and such assistants as he may need and fix their compensation. He may delegate to his chief clerk authority in his absence to certify estimates to the comptroller, to sign orders for the transfer of convicts, to approve vouchers covering expenditures made by the wardens and by the medical superintendents of the Matteawan State Hospital for Insane Criminals and the Dannemora Hospital for Insane Convicts, when completed and ready for occupancy, and to conduct investigations in matters pertaining to the institutions under his charge. The chief clerk may administer oaths and take affidavits in all matters relating to the affairs of the state prisons.

[The first sentence is the first sentence of § 40 of R. S., pt. IV, chap. 3. tit. II, as amended by L. 1889, chap. 382.

The provision of the present law relating to the delegation of power to the chief clerk is as follows:

"The superintendent of state prisons may delegate to his clerk authority to certify, in the absence of the superintendent, estimates to the comptroller, to sign orders for the transfer of convicts, and to sign orders for the discharge of insane criminals, whose term of imprisonment has expired."

Section 65 of the present statute authorizes the chief clerk to administer oaths and take affidavits.]

§ 143. General powers and duties of superintendent.— The superintendent of state prisons shall:

1. Have the general supervision, management and control of the state prisons and the convicts therein, and of all matters relating to their government, discipline, contracts and fiscal concerns.

2. Inquire into all matters connected with such prisons.

3. Makes rules and regulations, not inconsistent with law, for the government and discipline of each prison and of the officers and employes thereof, except the clerks and assistant clerks, and cause the same to be recorded by the clerk of the prison and a printed copy thereof to be furnished to each officer thereof upon his appointment.

4. Prescribe a uniform system of accounts and records to be kept at each prison.

5. Have power to require reports from the warden or other officers in relation to their conduct as such officers.

6. Inquire into any improper conduct alleged to have been committed by an officer or employe of either of such prisons.

7. Have power to take proofs and hear testimony, under oath, in any investigation or inquiry which he is authorized to conduct, and may issue subpoenas for the attendance of witnesses and the production of papers thereat.

8. Have power to administer oaths and take acknowledgments in all matters relating to the state prisons.

[R. S., pt. IV, chap. 3, tit. II, § 40, as amended by
L. 1889, chap. 382.

The several powers and duties are arranged in subdivisions for convenience of reference.

Subdivisions 1, 2, 3, 5 and 6 are proposed enactments of similar provisions in § 40 of the present law, without change.

Subdivision 4 is derived from a sentence contained in such § 40, which reads as follows: "He shall also prescribe a system of accounts and records to be kept at each prison, which system shall be uniform at all of said prisons, and he may also make rules and regulations for a record of photographs and other means of identifying each convict received into said prisons." The latter part of such sentence relating to photographs and the identification of convicts is superseded by the Bertillon system of identification.

Subdivision 7 is taken from the following sentence of such § 40: "The superintendent of state prisons shall have power to enquire into any improper conduct which may be alleged to have been committed by the agent and warden or other officer of either of the said prisons, and for that purpose to issue subpoenas to compel the attendance of witnesses, and the production before him of books, writings and papers in the same manner and with the like effect and subject to the same penalties for disobedience as in cases of trials before justices of the peace, and to examine in person or by attorney all persons who may be brought before him as such witnesses." We have omitted the reference to penalties for disobedience of subpoenas. Sections 852-856 of the code of civil procedure authorizes any person who has the power to "hear, try or determine a matter" to issue subpoenas and compel the attendance of witnesses and to punish a witness who refuses to answer pertinent questions.

Such sections being applicable to hearings before the superintendent, it is unnecessary to re-enact a part of the sentence above quoted.

Subdivision 8 is a similar power to that granted by the first sentence of § 65 of the former law.]

§ 144. Annual report of the superintendent.— The superintendent of state prisons shall, on or before the tenth day of January in each year, report to the legislature in writing the condition of each of the prisons for the year ending with the last day of the previous September, specifying the number of convicts confined during such year, and for what offenses; the number transferred from any prison and for what reasons; the moral, intellectual and physical condition of the prisoners and how employed; the amount of money expended during such year, and how, in detail; the amount of money earned during such year, and how, in detail; the amount paid into the treasury during such year, and such others matters as may seem to him to be pertinent and proper.

[R. S., pt. IV, chap. 3, tit. II, § 41, as amended by
  L. 1889, chap. 382, without change.]

§ 145. Officers and employes.—There shall be in each prison:

1. A warden, physician and chaplain to be appointed by the superintendent and removed by him when, in his judgment, the public interests so require.

2. A clerk and assistant clerk, to be appointed by the comp-

3. A principal keeper, a store keeper, a kitchen keeper, a hall keeper, a yard keeper, and a sergeant of the guard, to be appointed and removed for cause by the warden, subject to the approval of the superintendent.

4. Keepers, guards, teachers and employes to be appointed by the warden, subject to the approval of the superintendent. The number of such keepers, guards, teachers and employes shall be fixed by the superintendent. He shall also determine the number to reside at each prison. There shall not be more than one keeper and one guard for each twenty-eight prisoners.

[R. S., pt. IV, chap. 3, tit. II, § 30, as amended by L. 1889, chap. 382, all except last paragraph.

For comparison we have inserted the part of such section from which the section of the revision is derived:

§ 30. The superintendent of state prisons shall appoint the agent and warden, physician, and chaplain of each of the said prisons, as provided in the constitution; and he may remove them from office whenever in his judgment the public interests shall so require. He shall designate such number of keepers, guards, teachers and other employes at each of said prisons as he may deem necessary for the safe-keeping and improvement of the prisoners or for the maintenance of discipline, and he shall also designate which of them shall reside at the prison. But the number of keepers and guards shall not exceed the proportion of one keeper and one guard to twenty-eight prisoners at each of said prisons.

1. The comptroller shall appoint a clerk of each of said prisons as provided by the constitution, and is authorized to appoint an assistant clerk of each of said prisons whenever in his judgment the public interests shall so require.

2. The agent and warden of each of said prisons shall appoint, subject to the approval of the superintendent of state prisons, a principal keeper, a store-keeper, a kitchen-keeper, a hall-keeper, a yard-keeper, a sergeant of the guard, and so many other keepers, guards, teachers and employes of such prison as shall be designated by the superintendent of state prisons as aforesaid,

and such agent and warden shall have the power to remove such subordinate officers and employes so appointed by him.

The most of the changes made are verbal.

The words "and removed for cause by the warden" contained in the third subdivision of the proposed section are new.]

§ 146. State detective.— The warden of Sing Sing prison may appoint, with the advice and consent of the superintendent, a state detective, who shall be located at such prison and be a keeper thereof.

[R. S., pt. IV, chap. 3, tit. II, § 34, as amended by
L. 1895, chap. 730, last two sentences.

The compensation of the state detective is prescribed in § 148 of the revision.

The present law provides that "There shall be at Sing Sing prison a keeper, who shall be known as the state detective * * * . The warden of Sing Sing prison is hereby authorized and empowered, with the advice and consent of the superintendent of state prisons, to appoint the state detective."]

§ 147. Qualifications of officers and employes.— No person shall be appointed as an officer in a state prison because of political services or partisanship. Each person so appointed shall be honest, capable and adapted to the work which he is required to perform and shall be over twenty-one years of age and a citizen of the state. No person shall be so appointed who is addicted to the use of intoxicating liquors. An officer or employe of a state prison who is intoxicated while on duty, shall be at once removed.

If an officer knowingly appoints a person to an office in a state prison, contrary to the provisions of this section, or fails to remove an officer or employe who to his knowledge has been intoxicated while on duty, it shall be a sufficient cause for his removal from office.

[The last paragraph is new. The remainder of the section is derived from R. S., pt. IV, chap. 3, tit. II, § 30, sub. 3. Such subdivision is as follows:

"No appointment shall be made in any of the state prisons of this state on the grounds of political partisanship; but honesty, capacity and adaptation shall constitute the rule for appointments, and any violation of this rule shall be sufficient cause for the removal from office of the officer committing such violation. No person under twenty-one years of age shall be appointed to or hold any office at any state prison, nor shall any subordinate officer be appointed at any of said prisons by the agent and warden, unless such subordinate officer is a citizen of this state."]

§ 148. Compensation of officers of state prisons.— The warden of each state prison shall be paid an annual salary of three thousand five hundred dollars, and his necessary expenses while traveling on official business. He shall reside at the prison in the house connected therewith, be provided with furniture, fuel and lights at the expense of the state, and be allowed rations from the prison stores for himself and family, and the services of such prisoners as may be required for household duty.

There shall be paid by the state to the physician, clerk and chaplain of each state prison, an annual salary of two thousand dollars, and to each assistant clerk, an annual salary, to be fixed by the comptroller, not exceeding fifteen hundred dollars. They shall have their offices at the respective prisons, and be furnished with fuel and lights therefor. The superintendent shall fix the salaries of the other officers of each state prison, not exceeding the following sums: The principal keeper, two thousand dollars;

the sergeant of the guard, nine hundred dollars; the kitchen keeper, store keeper, hall keeper and yard keeper, each twelve hundred dollars; each keeper, nine hundred dollars; each guard, seven hundred and eighty dollars; each teacher, three hundred dollars. The salaries of the other officers and employes shall be fixed by the superintendent, but that of the state detective shall not exceed the annual sum of eighteen hundred dollars.

The salaries of all officers mentioned in this section shall be paid monthly. Such officers shall not receive any perquisites or endowments for their services other than the compensation provided therefor by law.

[R. S., pt. IV, chap. 3, tit. 2, §§ 32, 33, 34, 35, as amended by L. 1889, chap. 382.

The sentence in § 32 which reads as follows is omitted: "The comptroller is hereby authorized to audit and allow from time to time all necessary expenses and subsistence of the agent and warden when necessarily traveling on official business, or when the attendance of such agent and warden is required at the seat of government, the necessity of such traveling and attendance to be decided by the comptroller, and the accounts therefor when so audited to be paid by the treasurer on the warrant of the comptroller."

This sentence seems unnecessary in view of the provisions contained in § 12 of the State Finance Law.]

§ 149. Official oaths.—The superintendent of state prisons and each officer of a state prison before entering on the duties of his office, shall take the constitutional oath of office and file the same in the office of the comptroller.

[R. S., pt. IV, chap. 3, tit. II, § 36, first clause, which reads as follows: "Within ten days from the time of notice of his appointment, the superintendent of state prisons shall subscribe and take the oath of office prescribed by the constitution and file the same in the office of the secretary of state, and shall be in all respects subject to the provisions of the sixth title of chapter five of the first part of the revised statutes."

The reference to the revised statutes is now to the Public Officers Law, which repealed all of chap. 5 of pt. I of the revised statutes. The manner and form of taking the oath are prescribed by Public Officers L., § 10.

Section 37 of R. S., pt. IV, chap. 3, tit. II, requires all prison officers to take and subscribe the constitutional oath of office, which must be filed in the office of the comptroller.]

§ 150. Undertakings.—The superintendent of state prisons shall execute an official undertaking in the sum of twenty-five thousand dollars, with sureties approved by the comptroller. The warden of each state prison and every other officer, when required to perform the duties of the warden, shall execute an official undertaking, with sureties approved by the superintendent and comptroller, in the sum of fifty thousand dollars. The comptroller may require a new undertaking to be executed at any time.

Each clerk and assistant clerk of a state prison shall execute an undertaking, with sufficient sureties approved by the comptroller, in the sum of six thousand dollars. Each principal keeper, store keeper, kitchen keeper, hall keeper and yard keeper of a state prison shall execute an undertaking with sufficient sureties approved by the superintendent of state prisons, in the sum of five thousand dollars. All such undertakings shall be filed in the office of the comptroller.

[R. S., pt. IV, chap. 3, tit. II, §§ 36 (in part), 38, 39,
    as amended by L. 1889, chap. 382.

Public Officers Law, §§ 11-13, provide the method of executing an official undertaking and prescribe the effect of a failure to so execute. We have, therefore, omitted the part of the sections here revised, relating to the form and effect of the undertakings required. The undertaking of the clerk is made six thousand dollars. No undertaking is now required of the assistant clerk. His duties are such that an undertaking should be required of him as of the clerk.]

§ 151. General duties of warden.—The warden of each state prison shall:

1. Attend regularly at such prison, and, subject to the authority of the superintendent, have the general supervision, government and control of the prison, of the subordinate officers and employes thereof, of the prisoners therein, and of the fiscal and business concerns thereof.

2. Observe and enforce the rules and regulations of the superintendent.

3. Examine diligently into the state of the prison, the conduct of the officers and employes thereof, and into the health, condition and safe-keeping of the prisoners.

4. Inquire into the justice of complaints made by the prisoners, relative to their provisions, clothing or treatment.

5. Make necessary rules and regulations for the government of the prison, not inconsistent with law or the rules and regulations of the superintendent. He shall cause such rules and regulations to be entered in a book and copies thereof to be printed and distributed to each of the officers and employes upon their appointment.

6. Cause a daily journal to be kept of the proceedings of the prison, which shall include each infraction known by him of the rules and regulations of the prison by an officer, the nature and

amount of each punishment inflicted upon a prisoner, and by whom, and a memorandum of every well-founded complaint, made by a prisoner relative to bad or insufficient food, want of clothing, and cruel or unjust treatment by an officer. Such journal shall be open at all times to the examination of the superintendent and the commission, or an officer or member thereof.

[Subdivisions 1-5 are a revision of § 42 of R. S., pt. IV, chap. 3, tit. II, as amended by L. 1889, chap. 382. No intended change has been made.

Subdivision 6 is derived from § 43 of such statutes.]

§ 152. General duties of clerk.—The clerk of each state prison shall:

1. Reside within one mile of the prison.

2. Conform to the disciplinary rules of the prison and perform his duties as prescribed by the comptroller.

3. Enter in a book, under appropriate columns, the name of each prisoner in alphabetical order, his age, nativity, place of birth, occupation, complexion, stature, crime, court and county of conviction, term of sentence, number of previous convictions, places of previous imprisonment, date and manner of discharge therefrom and such additional facts as the superintendent may require to be so entered.

4. Make an entry of all money and other articles received by the warden from each prisoner, giving him credit therefor.

5. Make an entry in the books of the prison of all articles purchased for the prison, according to the bills received by the warden. If the articles received do not agree with the bills there-

for, in weight, quantity or quality, he shall note in such books the discrepancy and notify the warden thereof.

6. Keep an account of the financial transactions of the prison.

7. Preserve in the prison a set of all official reports made to the legislature respecting the same, and a set of similar reports in relation to each of the other state prisons, which shall be supplied to him by the superintendent.

8. Annually report to the warden of such prison on the first day of November the number of prisoners remaining in prison on the last day of the previous September, the number received during the year ending at such time, the number paroled, the number discharged by expiration of sentence, habeas corpus, pardon or otherwise, the number of deaths and escapes, and the number transferred to any other penal institution during such year.

9. Make an annual report, verified by his oath, to the secretary of state, on or before the first of December, stating the names of prisoners discharged or pardoned from such prison during the year ending with the last day of the previous September, and the same particulars in relation to such prisoners as are required to be stated in the warden's monthly report to the superintendent, and, in cases of pardon, the time when granted, the remainder of the term of sentence at the time of pardon, and the conditions, if any, on which the pardon was granted, and the state of health of each prisoner so pardoned at the time of his discharge.

The assistant clerk of each state prison shall assist the clerk in the performance of his duties, in conformity with the disciplinary rules and regulations of the prison, and under the direction of the comptroller.

[R. S., pt. IV, chap. 3, tit. 2, §§ 56, 57, as amended by L. 1889, chap. 382, revised and rearranged in subdivisions without change.

Section 57 is revised in the last paragraph of the proposed section.]

§ 153. General duties of physician.— The physician of each state prison shall:

1. Reside within one mile of the prison.

2. Attend daily during the proper business hours of the prison, and hold himself in readiness at all times to discharge his duties as such physician, whenever directed by the warden, unless by the direction of the superintendent he is otherwise engaged in the transaction of business on account of the prison.

3. Examine weekly the cells of the prisoners for the purpose of ascertaining whether they are kept in a proper state of cleanliness and ventilation, and make a written report to the warden in respect thereto.

4. Examine daily into the quantity and quality of the food furnished to the prisoners, and immediately report, in writing, all deficiencies therein to the warden.

5. Prescribe the allowance of food to prisoners undergoing punishment in solitary confinement and examine daily, and as often as required by the warden, into the state of health of such prisoners until released from such confinement.

6. Attend to the medical needs and prescribe the diet and treatment of the sick prisoners in the hospital, in the cells or elsewhere, and his directions in relation thereto shall be followed by the warden.

7. Have charge of the hospital, and keep a daily record of all admissions thereto, showing the name, age, nativity, place of birth, occupation, habit of life, crime, time of entrance and discharge from the hospital, disease, date of admission to the prison and the time confined in a county jail before conviction.

8. Report monthly to the warden the number of patients received into the hospital during the last preceding month, stating the facts in relation to each patient as shown by the hospital record, the number of deaths, the number of sick prisoners, not received into the hospital for whom he shall have prescribed during such month, and the number of days during which such prisoners, in consequence of sickness shall have been relieved from labor.

9. Annually report to the warden on or before the first day of November, the sanitary condition of the prison for the year ending with the last day of the previous September, with a condensed statement of the information contained in his monthly reports, and such other matters as shall be required by the warden.

[R. S., pt. IV, chap. 3, tit. II, § 58, as amended by L. 1889, chap. 382, without change, except as to the physicians' record and monthly report to the warden.

The present law requires the physician to keep a record of the prisoners " afflicted with scrofula before admission, scrofula during the first, second and third six months after admission to prison." This requirement is omitted, as, in the opinion of the prison physicians, it is unnecessary.

We have also omitted the requirement of reporting to the warden the kind and amount of medicines administered to sick prisoners.]

§ 154. General duties of chaplain.—The chaplain in each state prison shall:

1. Hold religious services in the prison, under such regulations as the superintendent may prescribe, and attend to the spiritual wants of the prisoners.

2. Visit weekly each cell in the prison.

3. Visit the prisoners in their cells for the purpose of giving them religious and moral instruction, and devote at least one hour in each week day and the afternoon of each Sunday to such instruction.

4. Furnish at the expense of the state a Bible to each prisoner who requests it.

5. Have charge of the library, and see that no improper books are introduced into the cells of the prisoners, and if any such book shall be found in the cells or in the possession of a prisoner take and return it to the warden.

6. Visit daily the sick in the hospital.

7. Report in writing quarterly to the warden the number of prisoners instructed during the last quarter, the branches of such instruction, the text-books used therein, the progress made by the prisoners, noting especially cases of unusual progress.

8. Annually on or before the first day of November, report in writing, under oath, to the warden, the religious and moral conduct of the prisoners during the year ending with the last day of the previous September, stating what services he shall have performed and the results of his instruction, and setting forth, as far as practicable, in tabular form, the number of prisoners in the prison on the last day of the previous September, the name and age at conviction of each, the number born in the United States, foreigners, birthplace of parents, the number able to read, read only, to read and write, well educated, classically educated, temperate, intemperate, healthy, whether employed at the time of the commission of the crime, county where convicted, occupation, sentence, how many times recommitted and social state.

[R. S., pt. IV, chap. 3, tit. II, § 59, as amended by
L. 1889, chap. 382, without change in substance.]

§ 155. General duties of principal keeper.— The principal keeper of each state prison shall enter in a time book, the name of each officer, keeper, guard and employe of the prison, except the warden, and shall daily mark therein the number of hours of service performed by each officer, keeper, guard or employe. At the end of each month, he shall report to the warden a verified summary statement of such record.

In the absence of the warden he shall have all the powers and shall perform the duties of the warden, except those relating to the financial affairs of the prison.

[R. S., pt. IV, chap. 3, tit. II, § 60, as amended by
L. 1889, chap. 382. The last sentence is new.]

§ 156. **General duties of storekeeper.**—The storekeeper of each state prison shall:

1. Have charge of and keep in a safe place all articles purchased for the maintenance of the prison.

2. Compare all purchases with the bills therefor furnished to him by the warden and note all discrepancies in quantity, or quality.

3. Make an entry of all articles received by him for the use of the prison.

4. Make an entry of each requisition upon him, showing the quantity and quality of the articles desired, on whose order and where sent. Articles shall not be delivered by him to any person, except upon the written requisition of the warden, principal keeper or kitchen keeper, or in their absence, of the persons acting as such. All such requisitions shall be filed in his office.

5. Make out, at the end of each month, a sworn statement of the quantity and quality of articles delivered on requisitions, to whom delivered and the quantity and quality then on hand and the value thereof. Such statement shall be delivered to the warden, examined by him and if found correct, he shall attach thereto his certificate to such effect.

[R. S., pt. IV, chap. 3, tit. II, § 61, as amended by
L. 1889, rearranged but not changed.]

§ 157. **General duties of kitchen keeper.**—The kitchen keeper of each state prison shall keep an account of the articles received on his requisition from the store keeper, the quantity prepared as food for the use of the prison and the articles sent to the hospital. He shall make a verified report at the end of each month to the warden of the amount of such goods received and consumed during the month, and the amount on hand at such time.

[R. S., pt. IV, chap. 3, tit. II, § 62, as amended by L. 1889, chap. 382, without change.]

ARTICLE VII.

STATE PRISONS; FINANCES AND PROPERTY.

Section 160. Warden, chief financial officer.

161. Warden's books of accounts.

162. Collection of debts.

163. Payments by warden or other officer.

164. Monthly estimates of expenses.

165. Contracts for supplies.

166. Vouchers.

167. Weekly bank deposits; statement of warden.

168. Monthly reports of warden to comptroller.

169. Annual report of warden to the superintendent.

170. Estimates of the value of prison property.

171. Affidavits.

172. When bond of warden may be prosecuted.

173. Real property connected with the Sing Sing prison.

174. Real property connected with the Clinton prison.

[General note.—There are no changes proposed in the present law, by this article, except in form and language. The references at the end of the sections show their derivations.]

§ 160. Warden, chief financial officer.—The warden shall have control of the finances of the prison under his charge, subject to the direction and supervision of the superintendent. He shall conduct the fiscal transactions and dealings of such prison in his name as warden.

[R. S., pt. IV, chap. 3, tit. II, § 51, first sentence.
Such section is as follows: "All the fiscal transactions and dealings on account of each prison shall be conducted by and in the name of the agent and warden thereof, who shall have control over all matters of finance relating to such prison, subject to the direction and supervision of the superintendent of state prisons."]

§ 161. **Warden's books of accounts.**—The warden of each prison shall cause his accounts and fiscal transactions to be entered in books, provided for that purpose. Such books shall contain a regular and correct account of all moneys received and paid out by him by virtue of his office, including all moneys taken or received from convicts, or as the proceeds of the sale of property taken from them, and the names of the persons to whom and purposes for which payments were made. Such books shall be open for examination by the superintendent or the comptroller or a person authorized by either of them.

[R. S., pt. IV, chap. 3, tit. II, § 44, as amended by
L. 1889, chap. 382, without change.]

§ 162. **Collection of debts.**—The warden of each state prison shall enforce the payment of all debts due to the prison under his charge. Subject to the approval of the superintendent of state prisons, he may accept such security from any debtor, on granting him time, as he may deem conducive to the best interests of the state. He may, in his name of office, institute actions and proceedings in all matters relating to the prison, and may recover all sums of money due to him, as such warden, or to any former warden of the prison, or to the people of the state on account of such prison. In such an action or proceeding, the defendant shall not plead or give in evidence any offset or matter by way of recoupment or counter-claim, except for payments made and not credited, nor recover any judgment in such action or proceeding against such warden, other than for costs and disbursements therein.

[R. S., pt. IV, chap. 3, tit. II, § 51, as amended by L. 1889, chap. 382, all except the first sentence, which is included in § 160 of the revision. The part of such § 51 from which this section of the revision is derived is as follows:

" Such agent and warden shall be capable in law of suing in all courts and places, and in all matters concerning the prison, by his name of office, and by that name shall be authorized to sue for and recover all sums of money due from any person to any former agent, or agent and warden of the prison, or to the people of this state on account of such prison. But it shall not be lawful in any such suit or action for any defendant or defendants to plead or give in evidence any offset or matter by way of recoupment or counter-claim (except for payments made, and not credited to such defendant or defendants), or to recover any judgment against such agent and warden in such suit or action other than for the costs and disbursements therein. Each agent and warden shall enforce the payment of all debts due to the prison under his charge as soon and with as little delay as possible, but with the approbation of the superintendent of state prisons, and subject to such approbation he may accept any security from any debtor on granting him time, that he may deem conducive to the interests of the state."

It will be noticed that the changes made are verbal.]

§ 163. Payments by warden or other officer.—No warden or other officer of a state prison shall give a note, draft or other evidence of a debt in payment for any article purchased for such prison, except a check on the bank, designated by the comptroller for the deposit of the moneys of such prison, and such checks and drafts as are authorized by law. No such warden or other officer in his official capacity shall sign or endorse a negotiable instrument for the purpose of having the same negotiated.

[R. S., pt. IV, chap. 3, tit. II, § 63, as amended by
L. 1889, chap. 382.

The words "signed by him or them individually or in their official capacity" are omitted as unnecessary. The last sentence of the proposed section is a substitute for the following clause: "Nor shall any such agent and warden, or any other officer, sign any paper as agent and warden for the purpose or with the intent of putting or having the same put in circulation for any purpose whatever."]

§ 164. Monthly estimates of expenses.— The warden shall make and submit to the superintendent on the first day of each month, an estimate in minute detail, of the necessary expenses for the support and maintenance of the prison under his charge during such month. The superintendent may revise such estimate by reducing the amount thereof, and shall certify that he has carefully examined the same, and that the articles contained in such estimate, or in such estimate as so revised by him, are actually required for the use of the prison. The superintendent shall thereupon present such estimate and certificate to the comptroller, who shall authorize the warden to make a draft for the sum thus certified, which shall be paid by the treasurer upon the warrant of the comptroller. The warden shall not make purchases on behalf of the state, not included in the estimate so certified, except for industrial purposes.

[R. S., pt. IV, chap. 3, tit. II, § 46, as amended by
L. 1889, chap. 382, without change.]

§ 165. **Contracts for supplies.**—The warden shall supply provisions and other suitable articles for the maintenance of the prison, either by contract or by purchase, as directed by the superintendent. If the superintendent shall direct that such supplies be obtained by contract, the warden shall cause notice to be published in a newspaper printed in the county in which such prison is situated and in such other newspapers and for such time as the superintendent shall direct, stating the particular supplies wanted, the manner in which they are to be delivered and the time during which proposals for furnishing the same will be received by such warden, subject to the approval of the superintendent. Contracts shall be made by the warden with those persons whose proposals in pursuance of such action are most advantageous to the state, and who shall give satisfactory security, approved by the superintendent, for the performance of their contracts, unless the superintendent shall deem it expedient to decline all proposals and advertise anew. The articles of food and the quantities of each kind shall be prescribed by the superintendent and inserted in the contract. All contracts made under this section shall be in writing and signed in triplicate by the parties. One of such triplicates shall be retained by the contractor, one shall be filed with the clerk of the prison and the other transmitted to the superintendent.

[R. S., pt. IV, chap. 3. tit. II, § 52, as amended by L. 1889, chap. 382, without change, except that by such section contracts are executed in duplicate.

It is proposed that contracts be executed in triplicate, one to be retained by the contractor.]

§ 166. Vouchers.—The warden shall take receipted bills for all goods purchased and services rendered for such prison, at the time of making payment therefor. The person to whom any such bill shall be paid shall make at the time of the payment an affidavit to the effect that the articles and services specified in such bill were actually furnished or rendered, as charged; that neither the warden, nor any person for him, or in his behalf, had any pecuniary or other interest in such articles or services or in the profits thereof; and to the best of his knowledge and belief no commissions, presents or profits, directly or indirectly, connected therewith, have been paid or promised to the warden or to any other person in behalf of or upon the request of the warden; that such bill represents the correct amount due, that the articles included in such account were sold at fair cash market prices, and that he has actually received the full amount in cash from the warden. Such affidavit shall be annexed to each bill paid.

[R. S., pt. IV, chap. 3, tit. II, § 53, as amended by L. 1889, chap. 382, without change.]

§ 167. Weekly bank deposits; statement of warden.—The warden shall deposit at least once in each week, to the credit of the treasurer of the state, in such banks as may be designated by the comptroller, all moneys received by him as such warden, except the proceeds of the labor of prisoners and of the sales of articles manufactured by them. He shall send a weekly statement to the comptroller and to the superintendent showing the amount so received and deposited, and when, from whom and for what received, and the days on which such deposits were made. There shall be attached to such statement the certificate of the proper officer of the bank receiving such deposits, showing the dates and amounts of such deposits. The warden shall annex to such statement his affidavit that the sum so deposited is all the money received by him from all sources of prison income, except proceeds of the labor of prisoners and of the above-mentioned sales, during the week and up to the time of the last deposit appearing in such statement. A bank in which such moneys are deposited shall, before receiving such moneys, file a bond with the comptroller, approved by him, in such sum as he shall deem necessary.

[R. S., pt. IV, chap. 3. tit. II, § 45, as amended by
L. 1889, chap. 382, without change.]

§ 168. Monthly reports of warden to comptroller.—On the first day of each month the warden shall make and submit to the comptroller an itemized statement of the receipts and expenditures of the prison under his charge during the preceding month, with proper vouchers. The comptroller shall enter his dissent on any voucher objected to by him, and return it to the warden, who shall cause it to be immediately corrected and returned. Such statement shall be verified by the affidavit of the warden to the effect that he has deposited in the banks designated by law for that purpose, all the moneys received by him, belonging to the state during such month; that such statement is a true abstract of all the moneys received and paid out by him as such warden, during such month; that the articles therein specified as purchased, were purchased and received by him at such prison at fair cash market prices, and paid for in cash; that neither he nor any person in his behalf had any pecuniary or other interest in the articles purchased and that neither he nor any person in his behalf has received, directly or indirectly, any pecuniary or other benefit therefrom in the way of commissions, percentages, deductions or presents, or in any other manner whatever, nor any promise of future payments, presents or benefits. The affidavit of the clerk of the prison shall also be appended thereto, to the effect that the articles specified in such statement as purchased were received at the prison, and that they conformed in all respects to the invoice of the goods received and entered by him, both in quality and quantity. The monthly reports of the principal keeper and store keeper to the warden shall at the same time be transmitted to the comptroller.

[R. S., pt. IV, chap. 3, tit. II, § 47, as amended by
L. 1889, chap. 382.

We have stated the contents of the affidavit to be attached to the warden's statement, rather than the form which it should assume. No change is thus made in the contents of the affidavit. The last sentence is a proposed re-enactment of a provision to a similar effect in §§ 60 and 61.]

§ 169. Annual report of warden to the superintendent.—On or before the fifteenth day of November in each year, the warden shall render to the superintendent a full report for the year ending with the last day of the previous September, containing a statement of the moneys received and paid out by him on account of the prison under his charge, all changes made in the offices of such prison during the year, and an inventory of the goods, raw material, and other property of the state on hand on the last day of the previous September. Such report shall be verified by the warden and clerk of the prison to the effect that it is just, true and correct. The annual reports to the warden, of the clerk, physician and chaplain of each prison, and such other matters as are required by the superintendent, shall also be then transmitted to the superintendent with the warden's report.

[R. S., pt. IV, chap. 3, tit. II, § 49, as amended by
L. 1889, chap. 382, without change.]

§ 170. Estimates of the value of prison property.— The superintendent may, whenever he deems it advisable, and shall, at least once a year, appoint two or more competent persons to make an estimate of the value of goods and other property of the state at each prison, of which an inventory has been rendered to him by the warden thereof. On or before the first day of January of each year, he shall transmit such inventory and estimate to the comptroller with such remarks in explanation thereof as he may deem necessary.

[R. S., pt. IV, chap. 3, tit. II, § 50, as amended by
L. 1889, chap. 382.

No change in substance is intended. The section has been rewritten and modified in form. For comparison we insert the section revised, in full:

"§ 50. The superintendent of state prisons may, whenever he shall deem advisable, cause an estimate to be made of the value of the goods and other property of the state, for which an inventory has been rendered to him by the agent and warden of either of said prisons, which estimate shall be made under oath by two or more competent persons to be appointed for that purpose by the superintendent, which inventory and estimate shall be transmitted to the comptroller of the state on or before the first day of January in each year, with such observations and remarks thereon as the superintendent may deem necessary to enable the comptroller to understand the same and to correct any errors that may be discovered therein."]

§ 171. Affidavits.—The warden, clerk, assistant clerk and principal keeper may take affidavits in all matters of accounts against the prison, and also in relation to fees of sheriffs in bringing convicts thereto.

[R. S., pt. IV, chap. 3, tit. II, § 65, as amended by
L. 1889, chap. 382, without change.]

§ 172. When bond of warden may be prosecuted.—If a warden willfully neglects or refuses to make or transmit a return, estimate, report or statement which he is required by law to make or transmit, the comptroller shall notify the superintendent of such delinquency, who shall cause the undertaking of the warden to be prosecuted for the recovery of any money in his hands belonging to the state.

[R. S., pt. IV, chap. 3, tit. II, § 55, as amended by
L. 1889, chap. 382.

The present law provides: "If the agent and warden shall willfully neglect or refuse to make any weekly or monthly return, estimate or statement, or to transmit any statement and certificate of such deposits to the comptroller," etc. We have modified the language of this sentence without any change in its meaning.

We have omitted the sentence: "The agent and warden of a state prison shall be liable to indictment and punishment for any wilful neglect of duty, or for any malpractice in the discharge of the duties of his office." Section 154 of the Penal Code makes malfeasance in office a misdemeanor.]

§ 173. Real property connected with the Sing Sing state prison.—The warden of Sing Sing prison shall continue to have charge of the farm and premises on which the same is situated and may rent or otherwise use or improve the same to the best advantage of the state, but no lease shall be made for a longer term than three years.

[R. S., pt. IV, chap. 3, tit. 2, § 68, as amended by
L. 1889, chap. 382, without change.]

§ 174. Real property connected with the Clinton prison.—All lands belonging to the state, or which may hereafter become the property thereof, situated within ten miles of Clinton prison shall be withdrawn from sale and shall be retained by the state for the use of such prison.

The warden of Clinton prison is authorized to appropriate to the use thereof all waters upon the tract purchased for the establishment of such prison, or upon the lands retained by the state for the use of such prison; and any person claiming damages in consequence of such appropriation, shall, within six months thereafter make application to the county judge of the county of Clinton, who shall appoint three commissioners not interested in the lands through which the stream or streams of water so appropriated may have previously run, who shall personally examine the lands of the applicant and make an estimate of the damages he has sustained by reason of such appropriation. Such estimate shall be in writing, subscribed and sworn to by such commissioners and submitted to the county judge of such county who may make an order affirming such estimate or rejecting it and appointing three other commissioners to make a new estimate of such damages. An appeal may be taken from such order within thirty days after the date thereof to the appellate division of the supreme court, by the state or the person making such application, and the decision of such court shall be final. Such estimate and the order of affirmance shall be transmitted to the comptroller, who shall thereupon draw his warrant upon the treasurer for the payment of the estimated damages out of the funds appropriated for the maintenance of such prison.

[R. S., pt. IV, chap. 3, tit. II, § 66, as amended by
L. 1889, chap. 382, and § 67, as amended by
L. 1897, chap. 216.

The only change made is in the procedure where it is desired to appropriate the use of waters for the prison.]

ARTICLE VIII.

STATE PRISONS. — SENTENCE, RECEPTION, TRANSPORTATION AND TRANSFER OF PRISONERS.

Section 180. To what prisons convicts to be sentenced.

181. Reception of convict whose death sentence is commuted.

182. Delivery of prisoner to prison.

183. Transportation of prisoners.

184. Liquors not to be sold or given to a prisoner being transported to a state prison.

185. Compensation of sheriffs for transportation of prisoners.

186. Compensation of sheriffs, how paid.

187. Transfer of prisoners.

188. Warden's daily report of prisoners received and discharged.

[General note.—The laws included in this article are revised without change in substance, except the provisions relating to giving liquor to prisoners being transported to a state prison, and that the warden's report to the superintendent of prisoners received and discharged, is to be made daily. This conforms with the present practice according to the rules and regulations of the superintendent.]

§ 180. To what prisons convicts to be sentenced.—All male convicts sentenced to imprisonment in a state prison in the first and second judicial districts shall be sentenced to the Sing S'ng prison, in the third and fourth judicial districts, to the Clinton prison, and fifth, sixth, seventh and eighth judicial districts to the Auburn prison. All females sentenced to imprisonment in a state prison shall be sentenced to the prison for women at Auburn.

[All except the last sentence is a proposed re-enactment of R. S., pt. IV, chap. 3, tit. II, § 69, as amended by L. 1889, chap. 382. The last sentence is now contained in L. 1893, chap. 306, § 9.]

§ 181. Reception of prisoners whose death sentence is commuted.—The warden shall receive into the prison under his charge, on the order of the governor, any person convicted of a crime punishable by death, whose sentence is commuted to imprisonment for life or a term of years in a state prison, and confine such prisoners for such time.

[R. S., pt. IV, chap. 3, tit. II, § 72, as amended by
L. 1889, chap. 382, without change.]

§ 182. Delivery of prisoner to prison.—When a prisoner is delivered to the warden of a state prison, in pursuance of a sentence, the officer delivering such prisoner shall present to such warden the certified copy of the sentence received by him from the clerk of the court by which such prisoner was sentenced, and such warden shall give to such officer a certificate of the delivery of such prisoner.

[R. S., pt. IV, chap. 3, tit. II, § 71, as amended by L. 1889, chap. 382, without change; except that the words " and the fees of such officer for transporting such convict shall be paid by the treasurer upon the warrant of the comptroller " are included in § 186 of the revision.]

§ 183. Transportation of prisoners.—A prisoner sentenced to imprisonment in a state prison shall be transported thereto by the sheriff or a deputy sheriff of the county wherein he was convicted. All prisoners sentenced at the same term of a criminal court to the same state prison shall be transported at the same time, unless the court shall direct otherwise.

[The last sentence is derived from L. 1847, chap. 497, § 5. The first sentence is new.]

§ 184. Liquors not to be sold or given to a prisoner being transported to a state prison.—A sheriff or deputy sheriff who sells or gives, or allows any other person to sell or give distilled or rectified spirits, wine, fermented and malt liquors to a prisoner in his charge, while being transported to a state prison, or while such prisoner is in his charge drinks any such distilled or rectified spirits, wine, fermented and malt liquors is guilty of a misdemeanor.

[This section is new.]

§ 185. Compensation of sheriffs for transportation of prisoners.—There shall be paid to sheriffs of counties for transporting prisoners from county jails to state prisons mileage at the following rates: For conveying one prisoner, fifteen cents for each mile actually traveled; for two prisoners, twenty-five cents for each such mile; for three prisoners, thirty cents for each such mile, and for four or more, eight cents each for each such mile.

There shall also be paid for the maintenance of each prisoner while on the way to a state prison, the sum of one dollar per day. The amount paid for such maintenance shall not exceed the sum of one dollar for every thirty miles of travel.

[L. 1877, chap. 128 (Gen. App. Bill), superseding
L. 1849, chap. 123.]

§ 186. Compensation of sheriffs; how paid.—On the delivery of such prisoners to the warden of a state prison, the sheriff or other person having charge of such prisoners, shall render to such warden an account of the number of miles traveled, the days spent in coming, and of the amount due therefor as prescribed by the preceding section. Such account shall be verified by the oath of such sheriff or other person to the effect that it is true and correct. There shall be attached to such account the certificate of the warden stating the number of prisoners delivered and the distance from such prison to the place of conviction. The account so verified and certified shall be audited by the comptroller, and paid by the treasurer out of moneys in the state treasury, appropriated therefor.

[This section is a proposed re-enactment of the parts of L. 1847, chap. 497, §§ 3, 4, and L. 1840, chap. 25, relating to the payment of compensation of sheriffs for transportation of prisoners to state prisons.]

§ 187. **Transfer of prisoners.**— Whenever a transfer of prisoners from one state prison to another is ordered by the superintendent, the warden of the prison from which such transfer is to be made, shall cause the prisoners to be sufficiently chained in pairs so far as practicable, and to be transported to the prison to which they are so ordered to be transferred, and to be delivered together with the certified copies of their sentences to the warden of such prison, who shall receive and keep them according to their sentences, as if originally sentenced thereto. The persons employed to transport such prisoners shall prohibit all intercourse between them, and may inflict any reasonable and necessary punishment upon such prisoners, for disobedience or misconduct. The necessary expenses of such transfer shall be deemed a part of the incidental expenses of the prison from which such prisoners are transferred. The necessary expenses of the transfer of any prisoner from a state prison to the Dannemora hospital for insane convicts, to the Matteawan state hospital for insane criminals, or to any other penal institution shall be a part of the incidental expenses of the prison from which the transfer is made.

[R. S., pt. IV, chap. 3, tit. II, § 73, as amended by L. 1889, chap. 382, without change, except as to the provision for the transfer of a prisoner to the Dannemora hospital for insane convicts, now nearly ready for occupancy.]

§ 188. **Warden's daily report of prisoners received and discharged.**—The warden shall report daily to the superintendent the names of all prisoners received in or discharged from the prison under his charge on that day, with such information relative to such prisoners as the superintendent may direct.

[By R. S., pt. IV, chap. 3, tit. II, § 48, as amended by L. 1889, chap. 382,
the warden's report of prisoners received and discharged was required to be made monthly. Under the rules and regulations of the superintendent now in force, such report is made daily. It seems unnecessary that the same report should be made monthly.]

ARTICLE IX.

STATE PRISONS.— SPECIAL PROVISIONS RELATIVE TO CARE AND TREATMENT OF PRISONERS.

Section 200. Cells, food and clothing.

    201. Instruction of prisoners.

    202. Removal of prisoners in case of pestilence.

    203. Removal of prisoners in case of fire.

    204. Duty of warden as to prisoner believed to be insane.

    205. When inquest to be held upon the body of deceased prisoners.

    206. Escapes.

    207. Money and property of prisoners.

    208. Money and clothing to be furnished to discharged prisoners.

[General note.—This article is a proposed re-enactment of the present statutes relating to the subjects included therein, without change, except in form and language.]

§ 200. Cells, food and clothing.—The prisoners in each state prison shall be kept in separate cells when not employed elsewhere, if there be a sufficient number of cells therein. Their clothing and bedding shall be of coarse material, manufactured as far as practicable in the prison. The prisoners shall be supplied with a sufficient quantity of plain and wholesome food.

[R. S., pt. IV, chap. 3, tit. II, §§ 85, 86, as amended by
L. 1889, chap. 382.

We have omitted the words "unless such prisoner be then released on parole" as found in § 85. The last sentence of § 86 provides that "the prisoners shall be supplied with a sufficient quality of inferior but wholesome food;" we have substituted the word "plain" for "inferior."]

§ 201. Instruction of prisoners.—The prisoners in each state prison shall be instructed in trades and other industries and in the useful branches of an English education. The warden of such prison shall appoint as keepers a sufficient number of persons qualified to give such instruction. Instruction in the useful branches of an English education shall be given to such prisoners, under the supervision of the warden or chaplain for not less than an average of an hour and a half each day, Sunday excepted, between the hours of six and nine in the evening.

[R. S., pt. IV, chap. 3, tit. II, § 84, as amended by
L. 1889, chap. 382.

We have here inserted the whole of such § 84:

"§ 84. It shall be the duty of the agent and warden of each of such prisons, so far as practicable and necessary, to appoint as keepers of such prison, persons qualified to instruct the prisoners in the trades and manufactures prosecuted in such prison or in other industrial occupations. Instruction shall also be given in the useful branches of an English education to such prisoners as in the judgment of the agent and warden or chaplain may require the same and be benefited thereby. The time devoted to such instruction shall not be less than an average of one hour and a half daily, Sunday excepted, between the hours of six and nine in the evening, in such room or rooms as may be provided for that purpose.]

§ 202. Removal of prisoners in case of pestilence.—If a pestilence or contagious disease breaks out among the prisoners in a state prison, or in the vicinity thereof, the superintendent may cause any or all of the prisoners confined therein to be removed to some suitable place of security, where such of them as are sick shall receive medical care and attendance; such prisoners shall be returned as soon as may be to the prison from which they were taken.

[R. S., pt. IV, chap. 3. tit. II, § 92, as amended by
L. 1889, chap. 382, without change.]

§ 203. Removal of prisoners in case of fire.—If a state prison, or a building contiguous thereto is on fire, and the warden apprehends that the prisoners may escape or be injured or endangered by such fire, he may remove such prisoners to some safe and convenient place, and there confine them until the necessity of such removal has ceased.

[R. S., pt. IV, chap. 3, tit. II, § 93, as amended by
L. 1889, chap. 382, without change.]

§ 204. Duty of warden as to prisoner believed to be insane.—If a warden believes that a prisoner in his prison was insane at the time he committed the offense for which he was sentenced, such warden may communicate in writing to the governor the facts upon which he bases his belief, and refer the governor to all sources of information with which he may be acquainted in relation to the insanity of such prisoner.

[R. S., pt. IV, chap. 3, tit. II, § 90, as amended by
L. 1889, chap. 382, without change.]

§ 205. When inquest to be held upon the body of deceased prisoner.—If the superintendent, a warden, physician or chaplain believes that a prisoner has died in a prison from any other cause than ordinary sickness, they or either of them shall call upon a coroner having jurisdiction, to hold an inquest upon the body of such deceased prisoner.

[R. S., pt. IV, chap. 3, tit. II, § 91, as amended by
L. 1889, chap. 382, without change.]

§ 206. Escapes.—If a prisoner escapes from a state prison, the warden thereof shall take all proper measures for his recapture and may offer a reward, not exceeding fifty dollars, for the apprehension and delivery of such escaped prisoner. Such reward may be increased with the consent of the superintendent, to a sum not exceeding two hundred and fifty dollars for each prisoner. The warden of a state prison may pay a reward not exceeding fifty dollars for the apprehension and delivery of an escaped prisoner, whether such reward shall have been previously offered or not. Any prison officer may arrest an escaped prisoner anywhere in the state, with or without a warrant.

All suitable rewards and other necessary expenses incurred in recapturing an escaped prisoner shall be paid by the warden out of the funds of the prison.

[R. S., pt. IV, chap. 3, tit. 2, § 89, in part, as amended by
L. 1889, chap. 382, without change.
The next to last sentence is new.]

§ 207. Money and property of prisoners.—The warden shall take charge of the money and other property brought to a prison by a prisoner, turn over the same to the clerk, and cause an entry to be made of the receipt thereof in the books of the prison. Such money and property shall be returned to the prisoner, upon his discharge or shall be paid or delivered upon demand to any person legally entitled thereto. Interest at the annual rate of four per centum shall be paid upon the amount deposited by or for the benefit of each prisoner from the time of making such deposit until such payment. Vouchers shall be taken for all payments made as prescribed in this section.

[R. S., pt. IV, chap. 3, tit. II, § 54, first sentence, as amended by L. 1889, chap. 382, without change.]

§ 208. Money and clothing to be furnished to discharged prisoners.—The warden shall furnish to each prisoner discharged from a prison by pardon or otherwise, or released therefrom on parole, necessary clothing, not exceeding twelve dollars in value, if discharged or released between the first day of April and the first day of November, and not exceeding eighteen dollars in value, including an overcoat, if at any other time, and ten dollars in money and a railroad ticket or tickets for his transportation from such place to the place of his conviction, or to such other place as such prisoner may designate at no greater distance than such place of conviction.

[R. S., pt. IV, chap. 3, tit. II, § 54, last sentence, as amended by L. 1889, chap. 382, without change.]

ARTICLE X.

STATE PRISONS; BOARD OF PAROLE; PAROLE OF PRISONERS.

Section 220. Application of article.

 221. Board of parole; meetings.

 222. Rules and regulations respecting the release of prisoners on parole.

Section 223. Record of prisoners under indeterminate sentences.

    224. Granting of paroles.

    225. Information from judges and district attorneys.

    226. Conditions of parole.

    227. Retaking of paroled prisoners.

    228. Fees and expenses.

    229. Absolute discharge of paroled prisoner.

    230. Articles and rules and regulations to be printed and distributed.

[General note.—This article is a proposed re-enactment of §§ 75-82 of R. S., pt. IV, ch. 3, tit. II, as amended by L. 1889, ch. 382. The board of parole of each prison is at present composed of the superintendent of state prisons, and the warden, principal keeper, physician and chaplain of each prison. It is proposed to eliminate the principal keeper and physician and substitute as members of each board, the president of the state commission of prisons and a member thereof, designated by it. By this change in the membership of each board, it is suggested that the prejudices or favoritism of prison officials will not influence the granting of paroles to so great an extent as is possible under the present law, and thus an objectionable feature of the existing system would be removed.]

§ 220. Application of article.—The provisions of this article are applicable to all prisoners confined in state prisons under an indeterminate sentence imposed as provided by law, and who shall have been confined therein for at least one year, and to all prisoners who have been transferred to such prisons from a state reformatory and who were sentenced to such reformatory for an indeterminate term.

[This section is new.]

§ 221. Board of parole; meetings.—There shall be a board of parole for each state prison, consisting of the superintendent, the president of the state commission of prisons, or a commissioner appointed by him, to act temporarily in his place, one other commissioner designated by the commission, and the warden, and chaplain of such prison. The superintendent shall be the president of each board and the clerk of each prison shall be the clerk thereof.

The board of parole of each prison shall meet thereat upon the call of the superintendent, but after the first day of January, nineteen hundred and one, they shall so meet at least once in four months.

[R. S., pt. IV, chap. 3, tit. II, § 75, and first sentence of § 76, as amended by L. 1889, chap. 382.

The present board consists of the superintendent, the agent and warden, the chaplain, the physician and principal keeper. See " general note " at beginning of article.

The last sentence is derived from the first sentence of § 76 of the present law, which provides that, " The board of commissioners of paroled prisoners for each of said prisons, shall meet at such prison, from time to time, as they shall deem necessary, or as they may be called to meet by the superintendent of state prisons."]

§ 222. Rules and regulations respecting the release of prisoners on parole.— The several boards of parole shall meet in the month of October, eighteen hundred and ninety-nine, upon the call of the superintendent, at his office in the city of Albany, and formulate and adopt uniform rules and regulations applicable to each state prison, not inconsistent with law, prescribing the conditions under which a prisoner may be paroled, the conditions under which he will be allowed to retain his liberty on parole, or be granted an absolute discharge, and regulating such other matters as may be necessary to a proper and uniform administration of the parole system. Such boards shall so meet in the month of January nineteen hundred and one, and annually thereafter in such month, for the purpose of revising and modifying such rules and regulations, if necessary, and for consultation on all matters relating to the parole system. The superintendent shall preside at all such meetings.

[This section is new.]

§ 223. Record of prisoners under indeterminate sentences.— The superintendent shall cause to be kept at each state prison, a full and accurate record of each prisoner confined therein upon an indeterminate sentence, containing a biographical sketch indicating the causes of the criminal character or conduct of the prisoner, and also a record of the demeanor, education and labor of the prisoner while confined in such prison. Whenever such prisoner is transferred to another prison, a copy of such record or an abstract of the substance thereof, with a certified copy of the sentence of such prisoner, shall be transmitted to the prison to which he is transferred.

[R. S., pt. IV, chap. 3, tit. II, § 77, as amended by L. 1889, chap. 382, without change.]

§ 224. Granting of paroles.—At each meeting of the board of parole a list of all the prisoners who have been imprisoned for at least one year and whose minimum term of imprisonment has expired, shall be furnished to such board by the clerk thereof, and the record of such prisoners kept by such clerk shall be produced to such board and examined by them. Such board shall make all necessary inquiry in respect to all such prisoners, and such of them as appear from their previous history, the nature of their crime and their conduct in prison, to be entitled to parole shall be called before such board for personal examination. If upon such inquiry and examination it shall satisfactorily appear to the board that a prisoner will probably lead an orderly and law-abiding life, if set at liberty, he shall be granted a parole.

[This procedure is not contained in the present law. We here insert the sections of the present law (R. S., pt. IV, chap. 3, tit. II, as amended by L. 1889, chap. 382), which provide a mode of action by the board in case of releases:

"§ 76. * * * At each meeting of said board held at such prison, every prisoner confined in said prison upon an indeterminate sentence, whose minimum term of sentence has expired, shall be given an opportunity to appear before such board and apply for his release upon parole, or for an absolute discharge as hereinafter provided, and said board is hereby prohibited from entertaining any other form of application or petition for the release upon parole or absolute discharge of any prisoner.

"§ 78. It it shall appear to said board of commissioners of paroled prisoners, upon an application by a convict for release on parole as hereinbefore provided that there is reasonable probability that such applicant will live and remain at liberty without violating the law, then said board of commissioners may authorize the release of such applicant upon parole, and such applicant shall thereupon be allowed to go upon parole outside said prison walls and enclosure upon such terms and conditions as said board shall prescribe, but to remain, while so on parole, in the legal custody and under the control of the agent and warden of the state prison from which he is so paroled, until the expiration of the maximum term specified in his sentence as hereinbefore provided, or until his absolute discharge as hereinafter provided."]

§ 225. **Information from judges and district attorneys.**—Upon application being made by the superintendent, the **presiding judge** of the court before whom the conviction of the prisoner whose minimum term has expired was had and the district attorney by whom the criminal action was prosecuted, or the district attorney of the county where the conviction was had, holding office at the time of such application, shall supply the board without delay with a statement of the facts proved on the trial of such prisoner, or if a trial was not had, the facts appearing before the grand jury which found the indictment, and of all other facts having reference to the propriety of granting or refusing a parole or absolute discharge as provided in this article.

[This section is new as applied to granting paroles by boards of parole. By section 695 of the Code of Criminal Procedure, the governor may require similar information in regard to prisoners making application for a pardon, commutation or reprieve.]

§ 226. **Conditions of parole.**— A prisoner on parole may be allowed to go outside of the prison walls and enclosure upon such terms and conditions as shall be prescribed by the rules and regulations made as provided in this article. Each paroled prisoner shall remain while on parole in the legal custody and under the control of the warden of the prison, until the expiration of the maximum term specified in his sentence, or until his absolute discharge as provided by law.

[R. S., pt. IV, chap. 3, tit. II, § 78, as amended by L. 1889, chap. 382, provides that when a prisoner is released on parole he " shall thereupon be allowed to go upon parole outside said prison walls and enclosure upon such terms and conditions as said board shall prescribe."

The last sentence of the proposed section is new.]

§ 227. Retaking of paroled prisoners.—If the warden of the prison from which a prisoner was paroled, has reasonable cause to believe that such prisoner has violated the conditions of his parole, he may issue his warrant for the retaking of such prisoner, at any time prior to the expiration of the maximum period of his sentence, which time shall be specified in the warrant. The board of parole or the superintendent may for a like cause, direct the warden of such prison to issue his warrant for the retaking of any such prisoner, and thereupon the warden shall issue such warrant.

Such warrant shall be issued to an officer of such prison or any peace officer, who shall execute the same by taking such prisoner into custody, within the time specified in such warrant. The officers shall forthwith take such prisoner before the county judge of the county, or a justice of the supreme court in the judicial district in which he is retaken, and such judge or justice upon satisfactory proof that such prisoner has violated his parole shall, by order, direct the return of such prisoner to the state prison from which he was paroled, and thereupon such officer shall return such prisoner to such prison, and he shall be confined therein until the expiration of the maximum term of his sentence, unless sooner released or paroled or absolutely discharged by such board.

[R. S., pt. IV, chap. 3, tit. II, §§ 79, 80, 81, as amended by L. 1889, chap. 382.

The present system of retaking is modified. By the present law the warrant for retaking a prisoner may be issued by any member of the board of parole.

The prisoner is then given an opportunity to appear before the board, and if he is found delinquent he is to be confined in the prison for a period equal to the " unexpired maximum term of sentence of such prisoner at the time such delinquency is declared, unless sooner released on parole or absolutely discharged by the board of commissioners of paroled prisoners."

The procedure before the judge or justice provided by the proposed section conforms to the procedure provided in case of prisoners released on parole from a reformatory.]

§ 228. Fees and expenses.—A prison officer shall be paid his necessary traveling expenses in executing such warrant. A peace officer shall be allowed the same fees for excuting such warrant as for executing a warrant of arrest at the place where such prisoner was retaken and if he transports the prisoner to the prison, he shall be allowed the same fees as are allowed by this chapter for transporting a convict from such place to the prison. Such expenses and fees shall be paid by the warden out of the moneys standing to the credit of the prisoner, if sufficient therefor, if not, the remainder shall be paid out of the funds of the prison.

[R. S., pt. IV, chap. 3, tit. II, § 80 (last two sentences),
as amended by L. 1889, chap. 382, without change.]

§ 229. Absolute discharge of paroled prisoner.—If it shall appear to such board that a paroled prisoner will probably live and remain at liberty without violating the law, and that his absolute discharge from imprisonment is not incompatible with the welfare of society, such board may issue to such prisoner an absolute discharge from imprisonment. Nothing contained in

this article shall be construed to impair the power of the governor of the state to grant a pardon or commutation in any case.
[R. S., pt. IV, chap. 3, tit. II, §§ 82, 83, as amended by L. 1889, chap. 382, without change in substance.]

§ 230. Article and rules and regulations to be printed and distributed.—This article and the rules and regulations adopted by the board of parole, as provided herein, shall be printed and distributed to the officers and employes of each state prison and the prisoners confined therein under an indeterminate sentence.

[This section is new.]

ARTICLE XI.

STATE PRISONS; PRISONERS UNDER SENTENCE OF DEATH; EXECUTION OF SENTENCE.

Section 240. Reception of prisoners under sentence of death.

241. Prisoners under death sentence to be returned to county jail when new trial is granted.

242. Death sentence, where and how executed.

243. Apparatus for executions.

244. Time of execution.

245. Who may be present at an execution.

246. Disposition of body of convict.

247. Warden's certificate after execution.

248. Disability of warden to execute death sentence.

249. Violation of article, a misdemeanor.

[General note.—Sections 505-509 of the code of criminal procedure relate to the execution of a death sentence by the warden of a state prison, and his powers and duties relating thereto. We have deemed it advisable to include in this article all the law relating to prisoners under death sentence and the execution of such sentence, and have therefore transferred such sections from the code of criminal procedure to the proposed law, without changing the substance thereof.]

§ 240. Reception of prisoners under sentence of death.—A prisoner under death sentence shall be delivered to the warden of the state prison designated by this chapter for the confinement of prisoners convicted of felonies in the judicial district in which the death sentence was imposed. The warden shall receive such prisoner and keep him in solitary confinement, until the infliction of the punishment of death upon him, as directed in the death warrant, unless he is lawfully discharged from such confinement. No person shall be allowed access to such prisoner without an order of the court, except his counsel, physician, a priest or minister of religion, if he shall desire one, the members of his family, and the officers of the prison.

[Code Crim. Pro., § 491, last two sentences, without change. The remainder of this section of the code relates to practice and is not re-enacted. It is not proposed that such section should be repealed.]

§ 241. Prisoners under death sentence to be returned to county jail when new trial is granted.—If a prisoner confined in a state prison under a sentence of death is granted a new trial, he shall be removed to the county jail of the county where he was convicted, by the sheriff of such county.

If such sheriff does not so remove him within ten days after such new trial is granted, the warden of such prison may cause him to be returned to such jail, and the expense of his removal shall be a charge upon such county and shall be paid in the same manner as other county charges.

[This section is new. It is obvious that a prisoner confined in a state prison awaiting the punishment of death, who is granted a new trial, should not be treated as a convicted criminal, and that the cost of his support and maintenance should be a charge upon that county in the same manner as a person awaiting trial for a capital offense. He should, therefore, be removed to the county where his new trial is to be had, without delay.]

§ 242. Where and how executed.—The punishment of death must be inflicted within the walls of the state prison designated in the warrant, or within the yard or enclosure adjoining thereto. Such punishment must be inflicted by causing to pass through the body of the convict a current of electricity of sufficient intensity to cause death, and the application of such current must be continued until such convict is dead.

[Code Crim. Pro., §§ 505, 506, without change.]

§ 243. Apparatus for executions.— The superintendent may cause electrical apparatus suitable and sufficient for the infliction of the punishment prescribed by this article, together with the machinery and appliances necessary therefor to be erected and kept in repair in each of the state prisons.

[L. 1889, chap. 36, § 1, without change.]

§ 244. Time of execution.—The sentence of death shall be executed by the warden of the state prison to whom the warrant is executed at the time fixed by him within the week specified in such warrant. No previous announcement of the day or hour of the execution shall be made, except to the persons who shall be invited or permitted to be present at such execution as provided in this article.

[Code Crim. Pro., § 504, last sentence, without change.]

§ 245. Who may be present at an execution.—The warden shall be present at the execution of a death sentence. He shall invite the presence thereat of a justice of the supreme court, the district attorney and sheriff of the county where the person to be executed was convicted, two physicians and twelve reputable citizens of full age to be selected by such warden. At least three days previous notice shall be given to such persons of the time of the execution. Such warden shall permit, at the request of the convict, not more than two ministers, priests or clergymen of any religious denomination to be present at the execution.

He shall also appoint, in addition to the persons above designated, seven assistants or deputy sheriffs who shall attend the execution. He shall permit no other persons to be present at such execution.

[Code Crim. Pro., § 507 (first three sentences), without change.]

§ 246. Disposition of body of convict.—Immediately after the execution, a post mortem examination of the body of the convict may be made by the physicians present at the execution. They shall make a written statement of the nature of any examination made, and present the same to the warden. After the execution and after the post mortem examination, if one be made, the body shall be placed at the disposal of the relatives of the deceased convict, if they so desire. If the body is not claimed by such relatives, it shall be interred in the graveyard or cemetery attached to the prison, with a sufficient quantity of quicklime to consume such body without delay. Religious or other services may be held over such body within the walls of the prison where the execution took place, but only in the presence of the prison officers, the person conducting the services and the immediate family and relatives of the deceased convict.

[Code Crim. Pro., § 507, in part,
without change, except that it is proposed that the post-mortem examination be made permissive. There is no longer reason for requiring absolutely a post-mortem examination in every case. It was originally required to ascertain the effect of an electrical execution upon the body of an executed convict.]

§ 247. Warden's certificate after execution.— The warden attending the execution must execute a certificate stating the time and place of such execution and that the convict was then and there executed in conformity with the sentence of the court and the provisions of this article and the code of criminal procedure. Such certificate shall be signed by all the persons present and witnessing the execution. There shall be attached to such certificate the physician's statement of the post-mortem examination. Such certificate and statement shall be filed, within ten days after the execution, in the office of the clerk of the county in which the conviction was had.

[Code Crim. Pro., § 508, without change.]

§ 248. Disability of warden to execute death sentence.—If the warden to whom a death warrant is directed is unable by reason of illness or other sufficient cause, to execute a sentence of death, the principal keeper or other officer of the same prison designated by the warden or the superintendent of state prisons, shall execute such sentence, and perform all the other duties imposed by this article upon such warden.

[Code Crim. Pro., § 509, without change.]

§ 249. Violation of article a misdemeanor.—Any person who shall violate or omit to comply with the provisions of this article is guilty of a misdemeanor.

[See last sentence of § 507 of the code of criminal procedure.]

ARTICLE XII.

STATE PRISON FOR WOMEN.

Section 250. State prison for women a department of Auburn state prison.

    251. Officers and employes.

    252. Salaries.

    253. Matron and assistant matrons.

    254. Storekeeper; compensation and undertaking.

    255. Clerk and chaplain; duties of woman physician.

    256. Sentence of women convicts; transportation.

    257. Children of women convicts.

[General note.—This article is a proposed re-enactment of L. 1893, chap. 306, providing for the establishment and maintenance of the state prison for women.]

§ 250. State prison for women a department of Auburn state prison.—For the purposes of government and management, other than as provided in this article, the state prison for women at Auburn shall be deemed a department of Auburn prison. The accounts, records and reports of such prison shall be kept separate and distinct from those of Auburn prison.

The warden of Auburn prison under the direction of the superintendent shall have the same management and control of such prison as is conferred upon him by law over the Auburn prison and the prisoners confined therein. The provisions of the preceding articles applicable to state prisons are to be applied to the state prison for women, except as they are inconsistent with the provisions of this article.

[The first and second sentences of the proposed section are derived from L. 1893, chap. 306, §§ 12, 13, without change.

The next to the last sentence is a proposed re-enactment of § 2 of such act, without change.

The last sentence is new.]

§ 251. Officers and employes.—The superintendent shall appoint a matron of such prison and he may remove her from office whenever, in his judgment, the public interests so require. He shall appoint and may remove a woman physician for such prison. He shall determine the number of assistant matrons, not exceeding one for each fourteen prisoners, and the number of guards, not exceeding four, sufficient for the safe-keeping and improvement of prisoners and the maintenance of discipline. The warden of Auburn prison shall appoint and may at pleasure remove, with the approval of the superintendent, such assistant matrons and guards.

[L. 1893, chap. 306, § 3. The provision for the appointment of a woman physician is new.

The present law provides that the superintendent " shall designate such number of assistant matrons, not exceeding one for each twenty prisoners, and such number of guards not exceeding four, as he shall deem necessary for the safe-keeping and improvement of the prisoners and the maintenance of discipline. Such assistant matrons and guards shall be appointed by the agent and warden of the Auburn prison, with the approval of the superintendent of state prisons. The agent and warden shall also have power to remove the assistant matrons, guards and other employes so appointed by him."]

§ 252. Salaries.—The annual salaries of such officers shall be fixed by the superintendent, and shall not exceed the following sums:

The matron, twelve hundred dollars; the woman physician, six hundred dollars; the assistant matrons, three hundred dollars; and the guards, six hundred dollars. Such salaries shall be paid monthly. Such officers shall not receive any compensation for their services in addition to such salaries.

[The salaries of the officers specified in the above section are fixed by L. 1893, chap. 306, §§ 4, 6. No change is made in these salaries. The provision relating to the woman physician is new.]

§ 253. Matron and assistant matrons.—The matron shall reside in the house connected with the prison, which shall be provided with proper furniture, fuel and lights, and she shall be allowed rations for herself from the prison stores. Each assistant matron shall board and lodge in the prison and without charge.

The matron shall, subject to the supervision of the warden of Auburn prison, be charged with the control and discipline of the inmates of the prison and direct the assistant matrons in the performance of their duties.

[The first sentence of this section is derived from L. 1893, chap. 306, § 5, without change.

The second sentence is now contained in the first sentence of § 6 of such act, and is not changed.

The last sentence is new.]

§ 254. Storekeeper; compensation and undertaking.—The storekeeper of Auburn prison shall be the storekeeper of the state prison for women and shall perform the same duties in respect thereto as he is required to perform in respect to the Auburn prison. He shall receive such additional compensation therefor as the superintendent shall prescribe, not exceeding the annual sum of five hundred dollars. In addition to the bond required as storekeeper of such Auburn prison he shall execute and file with the state comptroller a bond to the people of the state in the sum of twenty-five hundred dollars, conditioned for the faithful performance of his duties as storekeeper for the state prison for women, with sufficient sureties to be approved by the superintendent.

[L. 1893, chap. 306, §§ 4, 6 and 8.
Under the present law a separate officer may be appointed by the warden as storekeeper with a salary of not exceeding one thousand dollars. Under such law the warden has designated the storekeeper of Auburn prison to act as storekeeper of the state prison for women at an additional salary. The change made by the proposed section conforms with the present practice.]

§ 255. Clerk and chaplain; duties of woman physician.— The clerk and chaplain of Auburn prison shall be respectively the clerk and chaplain of such prison for women and shall perform the duties appertaining to such offices at such prison. The clerk shall receive as compensation an amount to be fixed by the comptroller, not exceeding the sum of five hundred dollars. The woman physician shall perform the same duties as to such prison as a physician of a state prison is required to perform in relation thereto.

[Under the present law, L. 1893, chap. 306, § 7, the physician and chaplain, respectively, of Auburn prison are physician and chaplain of the prison for women.

We have provided that a woman physician be appointed as physician of such prison.

The reference to the duties of the clerk of Auburn prison and provision fixing his compensation are not contained in the present law.]

§ 256. Sentence of women convicts; transportation.—A woman of over sixteen years of age, convicted of felony in any court of this state, and sentenced to imprisonment, shall be sentenced to imprisonment in the state prison for women. The clerk of the court imposing such sentence shall immediately notify the warden of Auburn prison thereof, and such warden shall cause such convict to be transported to such prison for women, in the company of at least one other woman; the expenses of such transportation shall be paid from the prison funds in the same manner as other expenses of prison maintenance.

[L. 1893, chap. 306, § 9, without change.]

§ 257. Children of women convicts.—If a woman sentenced to such prison, at the time of her incarceration under such sentence, is the mother of a nursing child in her care, under one year of age, such child may accompany its mother and remain in prison until such time as, in the opinion of the physician, such child can be properly removed therefrom and suitably provided for elsewhere. Such child may be committed to the care and custody of some relative or proper person willing to assume such care. If not so committed the warden may cause such child to be removed therefrom and placed in an asylum for children in this state. If the mother of the child had a settlement within the state at the time of her conviction, the cost of the support of such child in such asylum shall be a charge upon the county wherein she had such settlement; if such mother had no such settlement the support of such child shall be a charge upon the state in the same manner as a state poor child, committed to an asylum as provided in the poor law. If a child is born to such woman while in prison, such child may remain therein until removed as above provided.

If a woman when sentenced is the mother of and has under her exclusive care a child or children more than one year of age, who otherwise might be left without proper care and guardianship, the court sentencing such woman shall cause such child or children to be committed to an asylum provided by law for the reception and maintenance of destitute children, or to the care and custody of some relative or proper person willing to assume the care of such child or children.

[The first and last sentence of this section are a proposed re-enactment of L. 1893, chap. 306, § 11.

The remainder of the section is new.]

ARTICLE XIII.

DANNEMORA HOSPITAL FOR INSANE CONVICTS.

Section 260. Establishment and purposes of the Dannemora hospital.

261. Medical superintendent.

262. Medical superintendent as treasurer of the hospital.

263. Salaries of resident officers.

Section 264. Powers and duties of medical superintendent and assistants.

265. Monthly estimates.

266. Power of removal.

267. Transfer of insane convicts from Matteawan State hospital to the Dannemora hospital.

268. Transfer of prisoners in state prisons, reformatories and penitentiaries to Dannemora hospital.

269. Retention of insane convicts after expiration of their terms.

270. Discharge of insane convicts after expiration of terms.

271. Convicts on recovery, to be transferred to prison.

272. Certificate of conviction to be delivered to medical superintendent and copy filed.

273. Communications with patients.

[General note.—In this article, we propose a system for the management and control of the Dannemora hospital for insane convicts, which is now in course of construction.

The buildings for this hospital were commenced in 1896, under an appropriation made by chapter nine hundred and forty-nine of the laws of that year, and continued under an appropriation made by chapters three hundred and ninety-five of the laws of eighteen hundred and ninety-seven, two hundred and sixteen of the laws of eighteen hundred and ninety-eight. The hospital when completed is to be supported by the state as a part of the state prison system. It is proposed that all state prison and reformatory convicts, and all penitentiary convicts sentenced for felonies, who are now confined at the Matteawan state hospital for insane criminals, and who have at least six months of their terms to serve, be transferred to the Dannemora hospital. It is proposed that Matteawan should be used exclusively for the confinement of criminals who are declared to be insane before their conviction and of persons confined in penitentiaries and jails under sentences for less than one year.

We have applied the system of management and control now used at Matteawan as contained in article four of the Insanity Law, to the Dannemora hospital without material change.]

§ 260. **Establishment and purposes of the Dannemora hospital.**—The grounds and property located at Dannemora, in the county of Clinton and the buildings erected thereon, when completed, shall be designated as the Dannemora hospital for insane convicts. Such hospital, when ready for occupancy, shall be used for the purpose of confining and caring for such male prisoners as are declared insane while confined in a state prison or reformatory, or while serving a sentence of more than one year in a penitentiary.

[New.]

§ 261. **Medical superintendent.**—When the Dannemora hospital for insane convicts is ready for occupancy, the superintendent of state prisons shall appoint a medical superintendent therefor, who shall be a well educated physician of at least five years' actual experience as a prison physician or in a hospital for the care and treatment of the insane. A vacancy in the office of such superintendent shall be filled in like manner.

The superintendent of state prisons shall make by-laws and rules and regulations for the government of the hospital and the management of its affairs.

[New.]

§ 262. **Medical superintendent as treasurer of the hospital.—** The medical superintendent shall be the treasurer of the hospital, and before entering upon his duties, shall file with the state comptroller his undertaking to the people with sureties, to be approved by the superintendent of state prisons, to the effect that he will faithfully perform his trust as such treasurer. He shall have the custody of the moneys, securities and obligations belonging to the hospital, and shall open with some bank, in the vicinity of the hospital, to be selected with the approval of the comptroller, an account in his name as such medical superintendent, and immediately deposit in such bank all moneys received by him as such medical superintendent and treasurer, and shall draw therefrom only for the use of the hospital and in the manner provided by the by-laws and upon the order of the steward, specifying the object of each payment. He shall keep a full and accurate account of the receipts and payments, as directed by the by-laws, and of such other matters as the superintendent of state prisons may prescribe, and balance all his accounts, annually, on the thirtieth day of September, and within ten days thereafter deliver to the superintendent of state prisons, a statement thereof and an abstract of such receipts and payments for the past year. His books and vouchers shall at all times be open to the inspection of the superintendent of state prisons, who may at any time require of him a statement of his accounts and of the funds and property in his custody.

[New.]

§ 263. Salaries of resident officers.—The superintendent of state prisons shall, from time to time, determine the annual salaries and allowances of the resident officers, provided they do not in the aggregate exceed twelve thousand dollars; and the same shall be paid quarterly, on the last days of March, June, September and December, by the treasurer of the state, on the warrant of the comptroller, out of any moneys in the treasury appropriated for that purpose, to the medical superintendent, on his presenting a bill of particulars thereof signed by the steward, and properly certified by such medical superintendent.

[New.]

§ 264. Powers and duties of medical superintendent and assistants.—The medical superintendent shall be the chief executive officer of the hospital and shall:

1. Have the general superintendence of the building and grounds, together with their furniture, fixtures and stock, and the direction and control of all persons therein, subject to the rules and regulations adopted by the superintendent of state prisons, with power to assign their respective duties.

2. Appoint such number of assistant physicians, not to exceed one for each two hundred inmates or fraction thereof, as the necessities of the institution may require, and a steward, all of whom and the medical superintendent, shall reside in the hospital, and shall be known as the resident officers thereof.

3. Appoint such and so many attendants and other subordinate employes as he may think proper and necessary for the

economical and efficient administration of the affairs of the hospital, and prescribe their several duties and places, and fix, with the approval of the superintendent of state prisons, their compensation, and discharge any of them at his sole discretion; but in every case of discharge, so occurring, he shall, forthwith, enter the same with the reasons therefor, under an appropriate heading. in one of the record books of the hospital.

4. Give, from time to time, such orders and instructions as he may deem best calculated to insure good conduct, fidelity and economy in every department of labor and expense.

5. Maintain salutary discipline among all who are employed by the institution, and enforce strict compliance with all instructions and orders given by him, and uniform obedience to all the rules and regulations of the hospital.

6. Cause full and fair accounts and records of all his doings, and of the entire business and operations of the institution to be kept regularly, from day to day, in books provided for that purpose, in the manner and extent prescribed in the by-laws.

7. See that all accounts and records are fully made up to the last day of September in each year, and present the principal facts and results, with his report thereon, to the superintendent of state prisons, within forty days thereafter. The resident officers, before entering upon their duties as such, shall severally take and file in the office of the secretary of state, the constitutional oath of office. The first assistant physician shall perform the duties and be subject to the responsibilities of the superin-

tendent in his sickness or absence. The steward may personally purchase any supplies for the use of such hospital, but only in the name of the medical superintendent, and in each instance by his direction and not otherwise.

[New.]

§ 265. Monthly estimates.—The medical superintendent shall cause an estimate to be made monthly, in accordance with forms to be approved by the state comptroller, of all moneys necessary for the support and maintenance of the hospital, which may be required to supplement the deficiencies in the earnings thereof. Such estimate shall be submitted to and examined by the superintendent of state prisons, who, if he is satisfied that it is correct, and that the articles named therein are actually needed for the support and maintenance of the hospital, shall certify to the same, and on production of such estimate so certified, to the comptroller, he shall draw his warrant on the state treasurer for the amount thereof, and the state treasurer shall pay such amount to the medical superintendent of the hospital, out of any money in the treasury appropriated for the support of such hospital.

[New.]

§ 266. Power of removal.—The superintendent of state prisons may remove the medical superintendent, for cause shown, after an opportunity to such superintendent to be heard thereon, and such officer shall not be reappointed to the office of medical superintendent, or to any other position in said hospital.

[New.]

§ 267. **Transfer of insane convicts from Matteawan state hospital to the Dannemora hospital.**—When the Dannemora hospital for insane convicts is ready for occupancy, the superintendent of the Matteawan state hospital for insane criminals shall cause to be transported to the Dannemora hospital and delivered to the medical superintendent thereof, all male prisoners, convicted of felony, who are confined in such hospital upon a commitment thereto from a state prison, reformatory or penitentiary and who have not less than six months to serve of the term for which they were sentenced. The cost of such transportation shall be a charge upon the amount appropriated for the support and maintenance of Dannemora hospital.

The original certificates of conviction and copies of the medical certificates of insanity of the prisoners transferred shall be forwarded to the medical superintendent of Dannemora hospital, when such transfer is made. The names of the prisoners so transferred, with such information as the superintendent of state prisons may require, shall be forwarded to the office of such superintendent.

[New.]

§ 268. **Transfer of prisoners in state prisons, reformatories and penitentiaries to Dannemora hospital.**—Whenever the physician of either of the state prisons, reformatories or penitentiaries shall certify to the warden or superintendent thereof, that a male prisoner confined therein and sentenced thereto for a felony, is, in his opinion, insane, such warden or superintendent shall cause such prisoner to be transferred to the Dannemora hospital for insane convicts and delivered to the medical superintendent thereof. Such superintendent shall receive the prisoner into such hospital, and retain him there until legally discharged. The warden or superintendent, before transferring such insane prisoner, shall see that he is in a state of bodily cleanliness, and is provided with a new suit of clothing similar to that furnished to convicts on their discharge from prison. At the time of such transfer, there shall be transmitted to the medical superintendent of such hospital the original certificate of conviction and the certificate of insanity executed by the physician, which shall be filed in the office of such medical superintendent and a copy thereof filed in the office of the superintendent of state prisons.

[New.]

§ 269. Retention of insane convicts after the expiration of their terms.—When the term of a convict confined in Dannemora hospital for insane convicts has expired, and, in the opinion of the medical superintendent, such convict continues insane, the medical superintendent shall apply to a judge of a court of record to cause an examination to be made of such person, by two legally qualified examiners in lunacy, other than a physician connected with such hospital, qualified to act as medical examiners in lunacy. Such examiners shall be designated by the judge to whom the application is made. Such examiners, if satisfied, after a personal examination, that such convict is insane, shall make a certificate to such effect in the form and manner prescribed by the insanity law for the commitment of insane persons to state hospitals. Such superintendent shall apply to a judge of a court of record for an order authorizing him to retain such convict at the Dannemora hospital, accompanying such application with such certificate in lunacy. Such judge, if satisfied that such convict continues insane, shall issue such order of retention, and such superintendent shall thereupon retain the convict at Dannemora hospital until discharged as provided by law. The certificate in lunacy and order of retention shall be kept by the medical superintendent in his office, and one copy thereof shall be filed in the office of the superintendent of state prisons and another in the office of the state commission in lunacy. The costs necessarily incurred in determining the question of insanity, including the fees of the medical examiner, shall be a charge upon the amount appropriated for the support and maintenance of the Dannemora hospital, and be paid in the same manner as are other expenses of such hospital.

[New.]

§ 270. Discharge of insane convicts after expiration of terms.—The medical superintendent of the Dannemora hospital may discharge and deliver any patient whose sentence has expired, and who is still insane, but who, in the opinion of the superintendent, is reasonably safe to be at large, to his relatives or friends who are able and willing to comfortably maintain him, without further public charge; and such patient may, in the discretion of the medical superintendent, be provided with the whole or a portion of such allowances as are hereinafter granted to recovered convicts. Whenever any convict, who, by reason of his insanity, shall have been retained beyond the date of the expiration of his sentence, shall recover, he may be discharged by the medical superintendent, and such convict shall be entitled to ten dollars in money, suitable clothing and a railroad ticket to the county of his conviction or to such other place as he may designate at no greater distance. Any convict in the Dannemora hospital, whose term of imprisonment has expired by commutation or otherwise, and who is not recovered may, upon an order of the commission in lunacy, be transferred to any institution for the insane.

[New.]

§ 271. **Convicts on recovery to be transferred to prison.**—Whenever any convict, who shall have been confined in such hospital as an insane person, shall have recovered before the expiration of his sentence, and the medical superintendent thereof shall so certify in writing to the warden or superintendent of the institution, from which such convict was received, or to which the superintendent of state prisons may direct that he be transferred, such convict shall forthwith be transferred to the institution from which he came, by the medical superintendent of the hospital, or, if received from one of the state prisons, to such state prison as the superintendent of state prisons may direct; and the warden or superintendent of such institution shall receive such convict into such institution, and shall, in all respects, treat him as when originally sentenced to imprisonment.

[New.]

§ 272. Certificate of conviction to be delivered to medical superintendent and copy filed.—Whenever a convict is transferred to the Dannemora hospital, the warden or superintendent in charge of the prison, penitentiary, or reformatory from which such convict is transferred, shall cause a copy of the original certificate of conviction of such convict to be filed in the office of such warden or superintendent, and shall deliver the original certificate to the medical superintendent of such hospital; and whenever any such convict shall be transferred to any penal institution from such hospital, as hereinbefore provided, the medical superintendent shall deliver to the warden, or superintendent in charge of such institution, such original certificate, which shall be filed in the clerk's office of the same.

[New.]

§ 273. Communications with patients.—No person not authorized by law or by written permission from the superintendent of state prisons shall visit the Dannemora hospital, or communicate with any patient therein, without the consent of the medical superintendent; nor without such consent shall any person bring into or convey out of the Dannemora hospital any letter or writing to or from any patient; nor shall any letter or writing be delivered to a patient, or if written by a patient, be sent from the Dannemora hospital until the same shall have been examined and read by the medical superintendent or some other officer of the hospital duly authorized by the medical superintendent. But communications addressed by such patient to the county judge or district attorney of the county from which he was sentenced, shall be forwarded, after examination by such medical superintendent, to their destination.

[New.]

ARTICLE XIV.

CLASSIFICATION AND EMPLOYMENT OF PRISONERS.

Section 280. Classification of prisoners.

281. Powers of superintendent of state prisons relative to classification and transfers.

282. Prisoners to be employed.

283. Employment of prisoners in state prisons.

284. Employment of prisoners in state reformatories.

285. Employment of prisoners in penitentiaries.

286. Different grades of prisoners, how employed.

287. Employment of prisoners in state prisons upon public highways.

288. Labor of prisoners in county jails.

[General note.—This article contains a revision of existing statutes relating to the classification of and the manner of employing prisoners confined in the several penal institutions. The labor of the prisoners is to be employed as now. The changes proposed do not affect the substance of the present laws.]

§ 280. Classification of prisoners.—The prisoners in the state prisons, reformatories and penitentiaries shall be classified into three grades as follows:

Grade one shall include the least vicious prisoners who are susceptible of reformation and will probably observe the laws and maintain themselves by honest industry after their discharge.

Grade two shall include the more vicious prisoners who appear to be incorrigible, but are reasonably obedient to prison rules and discipline and competent to work without seriously interfering with the productiveness of their labor or of the labor of those in whose company they may be employed.

Grade three shall include the most vicious prisoners, and those who, because of insubordination, can not be employed without serious interference with the discipline of the prison or the productiveness of labor therein.

[R. S., pt. IV, chap. 3. tit. II, § 95, as amended by
L. 1889, chap. 382, without change.]

§ 281. Powers of superintendent of state prisons relative to classification and transfers.—The superintendent shall make rules and regulations for the classification of prisoners in state prisons and their promotion or reduction from one grade to another. He shall direct the separation of the prisoners of different grades within each prison. He shall transfer prisoners from one state prison to another whenever necessary because of the capacities of the respective prisons, or when it would be conducive to the health or reformation of the prisoners. He shall, as soon as practicable, so transfer such prisoners for the purpose of including all the prisoners of one grade in a single prison.

[R. S., pt. IV. chap. 3. tit. II, § 96, as amended by
L. 1889, chap. 382.

The present law is as follows:

"§ 96. The superintendent of state prisons may make rules and regulations for the promotion or reduction of the prisoners from one grade to another, and shall transfer from time to time the prisoners in the state prisons from one prison to another with reference to the respective capacities of the several state prisons, or with reference to the health or reformation of the prisoners, or with reference to including all prisoners of one grade as nearly as may be practicable in one prison, or may direct the separation from each other of the prisoners of different grades so far as practicable within each state prison."

It will be noticed that the changes suggested are verbal.]

§ 282. **Prisoners to be employed.**—The superintendent of state prisons, the superintendents, managers and officials of all reformatories and penitentiaries, shall, so far as practicable, cause all prisoners in such institutions, who are physically capable, to be employed at hard labor for not to exceed eight hours each day, except Sundays and public holidays.

[R. S., pt. IV, chap. 3, tit. II, § 98, in part, as amended by
L. 1889, chap. 382, and L. 1896, chap. 429.

Only the first clause in such section is contained in the above section of the revision.]

§ 283. **Employment of prisoners in state prisons.**—The prisoners in state prisons shall be employed, first, for the use and benefit of such institutions; second, in manufacturing articles and in the performance of labor for the use of the state and the public buildings, institutions and departments thereof; and third, in manufacturing articles for the use of the political divisions of the state.

[R. S., pt. IV, chap. 3, tit. II, § 103, as amended by
L. 1889, chap. 382, and L. 1896, chap. 429.

Such section reads as follows:

"§ 103. The labor of the convicts in state prisons and reformatories in the state, after the necessary labor for and manufacture of all needed supplies, for said institutions, shall be primarily devoted to the state and the public buildings and institutions thereof, and the manufacture of supplies for the state, and public institutions thereof, and secondly to the political divisions of the state, and public institutions thereof; and the labor of the convicts in the penitentiaries, after the necessary labor for and manufacture of all needed supplies for the same, shall be primarily devoted to the counties, respectively, in which said penitentiaries are located, and the towns, cities and villages therein, and to the manufacture of supplies for the public institutions of the counties, or the political divisions thereof, and secondly to the state and the public institutions thereof."

The first clause of this section is contained in the above section of the revision without change in substance.

The two following sections of the revision are also based upon this section of the present law.]

§ 284. **Employment of prisoners in state reformatories.**—The prisoners in state reformatories may be employed at hard labor, **or for industrial training and instruction, alone, even if thereby no** useful or saleable products are manufactured, **if such training and instruction can be more effectively given in such manner; or such prisoners may be employed in the same manner as prisoners confined in state prisons.**

[The present law contains no express provision similar to this, except in effect. See note to preceding section.]

§ 285. **Employment of prisoners in penitentiaries.**—The prisoners in each penitentiary shall be employed: first, for the use and benefit of such penitentiary; second, for the use and benefit of the county within which such penitentiary is situated, and in manufacturing supplies for the offices, public buildings, institutions and departments thereof; third, for the use and benefit of the political divisions of such county, and in manufacturing supplies therefor;

fourth, in manufacturing supplies for other counties and the political divisions thereof; and fifth, in manufacturing supplies for the state and the offices, public buildings, institutions and departments thereof.

[R. S., pt. IV, chap. 3, tit. II, § 103, as amended by
L. 1889, chap. 382, and L. 1896, chap. 429.

Such section is set out in full in the note to § 283, ante. The changes suggested are, for the most part, verbal.]

§ 286. **Different grades of prisoners, how employed.**—The primary or sole object of the labor of prisoners of the first grade shall be to fit them for self-maintenance by honest industry after their discharge from imprisonment. They may be employed at hard labor or for industrial training and instruction, alone, even if thereby no useful or saleable products are made, provided such training and instruction can be more effectively given in such manner.

Prisoners of the second grade shall be employed, as far as practicable, in manufacturing articles of value for use or sale, as provided in this chapter, or in the performance of labor for the institution in which they are confined or for the state or a political division thereof.

Prisoners of the third grade shall be given work or exercise which will tend to preserve their health, or they may be employed in the same manner as prisoners of the second grade.

[R. S., pt. IV, chap. 3, tit. II, §§ 99-101. Such sections are consolidated and rewritten. The substance is retained without change.]

§ 287. **Employment of prisoners in state prisons upon public highways.**—The superintendent may cause not more than three hundred prisoners in each state prison to be employed in the construction and improvement of public highways, within a radius of thirty miles from such prison and outside of a city or an incorporated village.

The warden of each prison, subject to the approval of the superintendent, shall designate the highways and portions thereof which are to be so constructed or improved. Such highways shall be under his control while such work is in progress. The state engineer and surveyor shall fix the grade and width of such highways and direct the manner in which the work shall be done. Such warden shall make all necessary rules and regulations for the proper care and control of the prisoners employed in such work, subject to the approval of the superintendent. He may, by direction of the superintendent, purchase machinery, tools and materials necessary for such employment.

[L. 1894, chap. 266, §§ 1-4. Under the present law the superintendent is authorized to purchase machinery, tools and materials.]

§ 288. **Labor of prisoners in county jails.**—Prisoners imprisoned in a county jail under sentence shall be constantly employed at hard labor, when practicable, for eight hours each day, except Sundays and public holidays. The board of supervisors of the county or the county judge may prescribe the kind of labor at which such prisoners shall be employed. The keeper of the jail shall account, at least annually, with the board of supervisors of the county, for the proceeds of such labor. Such keeper may, with the consent of the board of supervisors of the county, or the county judge, from time to time, cause such prisoners under his charge as are capable of hard labor, to be employed outside of the jail in the same, or in an adjoining county, upon such terms as may be agreed upon between the keepers and the officers or persons under whose direction such prisoners shall be placed, subject to such regulations as the board of supervisors or county judge may prescribe. The board of supervisors of a county may direct and make rules and regulations for the employment of such prisoners in building and repairing county buildings and town and county highways or in preparing the materials for the construction of highways for the use of such counties or to be sold to the towns, villages and cities therein. Such board of supervisors may cause money to be raised by taxation for carrying the provisions of this section into effect.

[County L., § 93, in part, as amended by
L. 1896, chap. 826.

Changes have been made in language but without intent to modify the present law. The last clause of § 93 is omitted as unnecessary.]

ARTICLE XV.

MANUFACTURE OF SUPPLIES IN PENAL INSTITUTIONS FOR USE OF THE STATE AND THE POLITICAL DIVISIONS THEREOF.

Section 300. Estimates of supplies required, to be made to commission.

301. Distribution and assignments of industries and labor.

Section 302. The board of classification.

        303. Modification of prices fixed by board of classification.

        304. Purchase of articles manufactured in penal institutions.

        305. List of articles manufactured in penal institutions.

        306. Requisitions.

        307. Certificates when articles cannot be furnished; bills and claims, when not to be audited.

        308. Payments for articles purchased; cost of transportation.

        309. Enforcement of provisions of article.

        310. Supplies manufactured by and labor of prisoners in penitentiaries.

        311. Prices for articles and labor furnished by a penitentiary to the county in which it is located.

[General Note.—The system of manufacturing supplies in penal institutions for the use of the state and its political divisions, as instituted by L. 1896, chap. 429, is retained in this article. We have modified the language of the present law and attempted to clear up apparent inconsistencies. Many matters of detail not found in the present law, are inserted.

For convenience of reference we here insert the sections of R. S., pt. IV, chap. 3, tit. II, as amended by L. 1896, chap. 429, which relate to the present system of prison manufactures:

" § 97. The superintendent of state prisons shall not, nor shall any other authority whatsoever, make any contract by which the labor or time of any prisoner in any state prison, reformatory, penitentiary or jail in this state, or the product or profit of his work, shall be contracted, let, farmed out, given or sold to any person, firm, association or corporation; except that the convicts in said penal institutions may work for, and the products of their labor may be disposed of, to the state or any political division thereof, or for or to any public institution owned or managed and controlled by the state, or any political division thereof.

"§ 98. The superintendent of state prisons, the superintendents, managers and officials of all reformatories and penitentiaries in the state, shall, so far as practicable, cause all the prisoners in said institutions, who are physically capable thereof, to be employed at hard labor, for not to exceed eight hours of each day. other than Sundays and public holidays, but such hard labor shall be either for the purpose of production of supplies for said institutions, or for the state, or any political division thereof, or for any public institution owned or managed and controlled by the state, or any political division thereof; or for the purpose of industrial training and instruction, or partly for one and partly for the other of such purposes.

"§ 99. The labor of the prisoners of the first grade in each of said prisons, reformatories and penitentiaries, shall be directed with reference to fitting the prisoner to maintain himself by honest industry after his discharge from imprisonment. as the primary or sole object of such labor, and such prisoners of the first grade may be so employed at hard labor for industrial training and instruction solely, even though no useful or salable products result from their labor, but only in case such industrial training or instruction can be more effectively given in such manner. Otherwise, and so far as is consistent with the primary object of the labor of prisoners of the first grade as aforesaid, the labor of such prisoners shall be so directed as to produce the greatest amount of useful products, articles and supplies needed and used in the said institutions, and in the buildings and offices of the state, or those of any political division thereof, or in any public institution owned and managed and controlled by the state or any political division thereof, or said labor may be for the state, or any political division thereof.

"§ 100. The labor of prisoners of the second grade in said prisons, reformatories and penitentiaries shall be directed primarily to labor for the state or any political division thereof, or to the production and manufacture of useful articles and supplies for said institutions, or for any public institution owned or managed and controlled by the state, or any political division thereof.

"§ 101. The labor of prisoners of the third grade shall be directed to such exercise as shall tend to the preservation of health, or they shall be employed in labor for the state, or a political division thereof, or in the manufacture of such useful articles and supplies as are needed and used in the said institutions, and in the public institutions owned or managed and controlled by the state, or any political division thereof.

"§ 102. All convicts sentenced to state prisons, reformatories and penitentiaries in the state, shall be employed for the state, or a political division thereof, or in productive industries for the benefit of the state, or the political divisions thereof, or for the use of public institutions owned or managed and controlled by the state, or the political divisions thereof, which shall be under rules and regulations for the distribution and diversification thereof, to be established by the state commission of prisons.

"§ 103. The labor of the convicts in state prisons and reformatories in the state, after the necessary labor for and manufacture of all needed supplies, for said institutions, shall be primarily devoted to the state and the public buildings and institutions thereof, and the manufacture of supplies for the state, and public institutions thereof, and secondly to the political divisions of the state, and public institutions thereof; and the labor of the convicts in the penitentiaries, after the necessary labor for and manufacture of all needed supplies for the same, shall be primarily devoted to the counties, respectively, in which said penitentiaries are located, and the towns, cities and villages therein, and to the manufacture of supplies for the public institutions of the counties, or the political divisions thereof, and secondly to the state and the public institutions thereof.

"§ 104. It shall be the duty of the superintendent of state prisons to distribute, among the penal institutions under his jurisdiction, the labor and industries assigned by the commission to said institutions, due regard being had to the location and convenience of the prisons, and of the other institutions to be supplied, the machinery now therein and the number of prisoners, in order to secure the best service and distribution of the labor, and to employ prisoners, so far as practicable, in occupations in which they will be most likely to obtain employment after their discharge from imprisonment; to change or dispose of the present plants and machinery in said institutions now used in industries which shall be discontinued, and which can not be used in the industries hereafter to be carried on in said prisons, due effort to be made by full notice to probable purchasers, in case of sales of industries or machinery, to obtain the best price possible for the property sold, and good will of the business to be discontinued. The superintendent of state prisons shall annually cause to be procured and transmitted to the legislature, with his annual report, a statement showing in detail, the amount and quantity of each of the various articles manufactured in the several penal institutions under his control and the labor performed by convicts therein, and of the disposition thereof.

"§ 105. The superintendent of state prisons, and the superintendent of reformatories and penitentiaries, respectively, are authorized and directed to cause to be manufactured by the convicts in the prisons, reformatories and penitentiaries, such articles as are needed and used therein, and also such as are required by the state or political divisions thereof, and in the buildings, offices and public institutions owned or managed and controlled by the state, including articles and materials to be used in the erection of the buildings. All such articles manufactured in the state prisons, reformatories and penitentiaries, and not required for use therein, may be furnished to the state, or to any political division thereof, or for or to any public institution owned or managed and controlled by the state, or any political division thereof, at and for such prices as shall be fixed and determined as hereinafter provided, upon the requisitions of the proper officials, trustees or managers thereof. No article so manufactured shall be purchased from any other source, for the state or public institutions of the state, or the political divisions thereof, unless said state commission of prisons shall certify that the same can not be furnished upon such requisition, and no claim therefor shall be audited or paid without such certificate.

"§ 106. On or before October first in each year, the proper officials of the state, and the political divisions thereof, and of the institutions of the state, or political divisions thereof, shall report to the said commission of prisons estimates for the ensuing year of the amount of supplies of different kinds required to be purchased by them that can be furnished by the penal institutions of the state. The said commission is authorized to make regulations for said reports, to provide for the manner in which requisitions shall be made for supplies, and to provide for the proper diversification of the industries in said penal institutions.

"§ 107. The comptroller, the state commission of prisons and the superintendent of state prisons and the lunacy commission are hereby constituted a board to be known as the board of classification. Said board shall fix and determine the prices at which all labor performed, and all articles manufactured and furnished to the state, or the political divisions thereof, or the public institutions thereof, shall be furnished, which prices shall be uniform to all, except that the prices for goods or labor furnished by the penitentiaries to or for the county in which they are located, or the political divisions thereof, shall be fixed by the board of supervisors of such counties, except New York and Kings counties, in which the prices shall be fixed by the commissioners of charities and correction, respectively. The prices shall be as near the usual market price for such labor and supplies as possible. The state commission of prisons shall devise and furnish to all such institutions a proper form for such requisition and the comptroller shall devise and furnish a proper system of accounts to be kept for all such transactions. It shall also be the duty of the board of classification to classify the buildings, offices and institutions owned or managed and controlled by the state, and it shall fix and determine the styles, patterns, designs and qualities of the articles to be manufactured for such buildings, offices and public institutions in the penal institutions of this state. So far as practicable, all supplies used in such buildings, offices and public institutions shall be uniform for each class, and of the styles, patterns, designs and qualities that can be manufactured in the penal institutions in this state."]

§ 300. Estimates of supplies required, to be made to commission.—On or before the first day of October in each year, the several officers, boards and commissions having charge of the purchasing of supplies for the offices, departments, institutions and public buildings of the state and the political divisions thereof, shall make an estimate to the state commission of prisons, of the amount of supplies of different kinds required for the use of such public buildings, institutions, offices or departments during the ensuing year. Such commission may prescribe the form of such estimates.

[R. S., pt. IV, chap. 3, tit. II, § 106, as amended by
L. 1889, chap. 382, and L. 1896, chap. 429.

See "General Note" at beginning of article. Part of the last sentence of such section is covered by the following section of the revision.]

§ 301. **Distribution and assignment of industries and labor.—** The commission shall assign to the state prisons the industries and labor which are to be conducted and performed therein, and assign to and distribute among the reformatories and penitentiaries the industries and labor which are to be conducted and performed in such institutions. In making such assignments and distribution due regard shall be had to the employment of the prisoners therein, in conformity with the provisions of the preceding article. No printing or photo-engraving shall be done in any state prison, penitentiary, or reformatory for the state or any political division thereof, or for any public institution owned or managed and controlled by the state or any such political division except such printing as may be required for or used in the penal and state charitable institutions, and the reports of the state commission of prisons and the superintendent of state prisons and all printing required in their offices.

Before assigning and distributing such industries and labor the commission shall consult with the superintendent of state prisons, in regard to the industries and labor that can best be conducted and performed in state prisons, and shall invite the superintendents of reformatories and penitentiaries to confer with the commission in regard to such assignments and distribution.

Reassignments and redistributions of industries and labor may be made by the commission whenever necessary for the general welfare of the several institutions. But whenever an industry has once been assigned, such assignment, if to state prisons, shall not be modified or limited without the consent of the superintendent of state prisons; if to a penitentiary or reformatory, without the consent of the superintendent or the board of managers thereof.

[R. S., pt. IV, chap. 3, tit. II, §§ 102, 104, 106, as amended by L. 1889, chap. 382, and L. 1896, chap. 429.

See General Note at beginning of article.

The present law authorizes the state commission to make assignments of industries to the several penal institutions and to make rules for the proper distribution and diversification of such industries.

The last sentence in the first paragraph is a proposed re-enactment of L. 1898, chap. 645, without change.

Except as above specified, this section is new.]

§ 302. The board of classification.—The comptroller, the state commission of prisons, the superintendent of state prisons and the state commission of lunacy shall continue to be a board of classification. Such board shall determine the prices for which labor shall be performed and articles shall be manufactured and furnished to the state or the political divisions thereof, except where such articles and labor are furnished to a county, or to the cities, villages, towns and school districts therein, by a penitentiary located in such county. Such prices shall be uniform and shall be as near the usual market prices for such labor and articles as possible. Such board of classification shall classify the offices, institutions, departments and public buildings managed and controlled by the state, and the political divisions thereof, and shall determine the styles, patterns, designs and quality of the articles to be manufactured therefor. So far as practicable, all articles used in such offices, institutions, departments and public buildings shall be uniform for each class, and of the styles, patterns, designs and qualities that can be manufactured in penal institutions.

[R. S., pt. IV, chap. 3, tit. II, § 107, as amended by
L. 1889, chap. 382, and L. 1896, chap. 429.

See " General Note " at the beginning of this article. It is not intended to change the substance of the present law by the revision.]

§ 303. **Modification of prices fixed by board of classification.**— If an officer, board or commission, having charge of an office, institution, department or public building of a political division of the state, required by this article to purchase supplies manufactured in the penal institutions of the state, is dissatisfied with the prices fixed by the board of classification for such supplies, application may be made to such board for a modification of such prices. If upon such application such prices are not modified or reduced to the satisfaction of such officer, board or commission, an order to show cause why such prices should not be modified or reduced may be granted by a justice of the supreme court of the third judicial district. Such order shall be returnable not less than eight days after the service thereof before such justice or a referee appointed by him, at a time and place specified therein. Such order shall be directed to the board of classification and shall be served upon the comptroller. Such justice or referee at the time and place mentioned in the order shall hear the facts relating to the application for a modification or reduction of such prices. After such hearing an order shall be granted affirming the determination of the board of classification or reducing or modifying the prices fixed by them as justice may require. Such order shall be final as determining the particular prices complained of. The justice making the order may allow costs in his discretion, to either party.

[This section is new. It is limited in its application to prices fixed by the board for articles purchased by the political divisions of the state. It is a hardship upon the counties, cities and villages of the state to compel them to purchase goods manufactured in a state prison, the prices of which are determined by a state board, if it appears that such prices are more than the goods required can be purchased in the locality of the county, city or village.]

§ 304. Purchase of articles manufactured in penal institutions.—The officers, boards and commissions having charge of the offices, institutions, departments and public buildings of the state, or the political divisions thereof, shall purchase from the penal institutions the articles required for the use of such offices, institutions, departments and public buildings which can be furnished by such penal institutions.

[R. S., pt. IV, chap. 3, tit. II, § 105, last two sentences,
as amended by L. 1889, chap. 382, and L. 1896, chap. 429.
See "General Note" at the beginning of this article.
The present law requires all purchases to be made from penal institutions, if the articles required are manufactured therein.
No change in effect is proposed by the revision.]

§ 305. List of articles manufactured in penal institutions.— For the information of the officers, boards and commissions having charge of the offices, institutions, departments and public buildings of the state, and the political divisions thereof, required by this article to purchase supplies manufactured in penal institutions, the superintendent of state prisons shall cause lists, showing, so far as practicable, the lines of supplies which can be manufactured in such penal institutions, to be prepared, and printed copies thereof to be mailed to such officers, boards and commissions. Such lists shall include the articles most commonly used in public buildings, offices, institutions and departments which can be manufactured to the best advantage in penal institutions, and shall, as far as practicable, specify the prices, styles, patterns, designs and quality as determined by the board of classification. The articles contained in such list shall be described or illustrated so as to furnish reasonably full information of the style, patterns, designs and quality thereof. There shall also be printed with such list full and accurate directions for making requisitions for such articles and such other information in regard to the purchase of, and payment for, such articles as the superintendent may deem expedient.

[This section is new. It is inserted to conform the law with the practice.]

§ 306. Requisitions.—All requisitions for articles manufactured and furnished by penal institutions to the officers, boards and commissioners having charge of the offices, departments, institutions and public buildings of the state and the political divisions thereof, shall be made upon the superintendent of state prisons. If the articles required for the use of the offices, departments, institutions or public buildings of a county or its political divisions, wherein a penitentiary is located, are manufactured in such penitentiary, under provisions made therefor as prescribed in this article, requisitions for such articles shall be made upon the superintendent or warden of such penitentiary, and copies of such requisitions shall be forwarded to the state commission of prisons, by such superintendent or warden, immediately upon the receipt thereof by him. If such articles are not manufactured in such penitentiary, requisitions therefor shall be made upon the superintendent of state prisons, as above provided.

If the articles called for by requisitions received by the superintendent of state prisons are not manufactured in or cannot be furnished within a reasonable time, by the state prisons, the superintendent shall at once so advise the commission, and if such articles are manufactured in or can be furnished by a reformatory or penitentiary, such requisitions shall be transmitted by such commission to the superintendent of such reformatory or penitentiary and such articles shall be furnished by him. The superintendent shall deliver to the secretary of the commission the original requisitions from which the secretary shall copy such part thereof as he may need for the information of such commission, after which such requisition shall be returned to the superintendent.

The warden of each state prison shall, on the first business day of each week, report to the commission the shipments of goods by such warden during the preceding week, showing the date of the requisition, date of shipment, name of officers, department or institution making the requisition, a description of the articles so sent out, and the quantity and value of each.

[This section is new in form. By § 106 of R. S., pt. IV, chap. 3, tit. II, as amended by L. 1896, chap. 429, the state commission of prisons is authorized to " provide for the manner in which requisitions shall be made for supplies."]

§ 307. Certificates when articles cannot be furnished; bills and claims, when not to be audited.—Articles required for the use of an office, institution, department or public building of the state or a political division thereof, which can be manufactured in penal institutions, shall not be purchased from any other source than a penal institution, unless the commission shall certify in writing that such articles cannot be furnished by any penal institution, upon such requisition, or that they cannot be furnished within a reasonable time, or that the quantity or value of the articles required is so small that it would not be to the interest of the state or county to furnish the same.

No bill or claim for furnishing articles to any office, institution, department or public building of the state or a political division thereof, which can be manufactured in and furnished by a penal institution, shall be audited or paid by the officers or board authorized by law to audit and pay the bills or claims against such office, department, institution or public buildings unless such certificate is attached thereto.

The officer or board knowingly auditing any such bills or

claims, contrary to the provisions of this section, shall be guilty of a misdemeanor and shall forfeit to the people of the state an amount equal to the sum paid upon such bills or claims so audited, to be recovered in an action brought by the attorney-general in the name of the commission.

[R. S., pt. IV, chap. 3, tit. II, § 105, last two sentences,
as amended by L. 1889, chap. 382, and L. 1896, chap. 429.
See " General Note " at the beginning of this article.
The present law is not changed in effect by the revision, although it is amplified and set forth more in detail.
The last sentence relating to the penalty for a failure upon the part of a public officer or board to make purchases as required by law, is new.]

§ 308. Payments for articles purchased; cost of transportation.—Payments for articles purchased from the penal institutions, as required herein, shall be made to the warden or superintendent of the institution in which such articles were manufactured. There shall be deducted from the amount charged for the articles so purchased, the cost of transportation thereof from the place of shipment to a point upon a line of public transportation nearest the place where such articles are to be used.

[This section is new.]

§ 309. Enforcement of provisions of article.—If the officer, board or commission having charge of an office, institution, department or public building of the state or a political division thereof, fails to comply with the provisions of this article, an application may be made by the state commission of prisons to a justice of the supreme court in the judicial district in which such public building, institution, department or office is situated, upon at least ten days' notice to such officer, board or commission, for an order directing a compliance with such provisions. If it shall appear upon the hearing of such application, that any of such provisions are not complied with, the justice shall make an order directing a compliance therewith, with such costs of the application as the justice in his discretion may impose. A failure to comply with such order shall be a contempt of court and punishable as such.

Such commission, or any of its members or officers having authority therefrom, may take testimony and inspect the accounts of any such public buildings, institutions, departments or offices for the purpose of ascertaining if supplies have been purchased contrary to the provisions of this article.

[This section is new.]

§ 310. Supplies manufactured by and labor of prisoners in penitentiaries.—The board of supervisors or other board or officer having charge of a penitentiary may provide, with the approval of the commission, for the employment of prisoners therein in the performance of labor or the manufacture of articles for the county wherein such penitentiary is located and for the political divisions thereof. Whenever provisions are so made the officers, boards and commissions having charge of the offices, institutions, departments and public buildings of such county and the political divisions thereof, shall purchase the articles manufactured in such penitentiary. If the articles required for the use of such offices, institutions, departments and public buildings are not manufactured in such penitentiary and are manufactured in other penal institutions of the state, such articles shall be purchased and requisitions shall be made therefor in the manner prescribed in this article.

[This section is new.]

§ 311. *Prices for articles and labor furnished by a penitentiary to the county in which it is located.*—The prices for articles or labor furnished by a penitentiary to the county in which it is located, and the political divisions thereof, shall be determined by the board of supervisors of such county. If such penitentiary is located in the counties of New York or Kings, such prices shall be fixed by the commissioner of corrections of the city of New York.

[R. S., pt. IV, chap. 3, tit. II, § 107, part of first sentence, as amended by L. 1889, chap. 382, and L. 1896, chap. 429, without intentional change in effect.]

ARTICLE XVI.

CONDUCT OF MANUFACTURING INDUSTRIES IN STATE PRISONS.

Section 320. Superintendent to distribute assignments of labor and industries to state prisons.

321. Disposal of manufacturing plants.

322. Purchase of machinery and supplies.

323. Monthly estimates in relation to manufactures.

324. Manner of purchasing materials for manufacturing purposes.

Section 325. Deposit of proceeds of labor of prisoners in banks.

 326. Weekly statement of deposits.

 327. Payment of drafts.

 328. Transfer of deposits to prison fund.

 329. Monthly statements of wardens relating to prison industries.

 330. Comptroller's report relating to prison industries.

 331. Superintendent's annual report.

[General note.—Sections 104, 111-115 of R. S., pt. IV, ch. 3, tit. II, as amended by L. 1889, ch. 382, relating to the manner of conducting the industries in state prisons are revised and included in this article. The changes, except as noted at the end of the sections, are verbal.]

§ 320. Superintendent to distribute assignments of labor and industries to state prisons.—The superintendent shall distribute among the state prisons the labor and industries assigned thereto by the commission. Such distribution shall be made according to the location and convenience of the prisons and of the public buildings, institutions, offices and departments to be supplied, the number of prisoners and the adaptability of the manufacturing plants in such prisons and the system used therein for the instruction, improvement and reformation of prisoners.

 [R. S., pt. IV, chap. 3, tit. II, § 104, in part, as amended by
 L. 1889, chap. 382, and L. 1896, chap. 429.
 See " General Note " at beginning of preceding article.]

§ 321. Disposal of manufacturing plants.—The superintendent may transfer industries assigned to state prisons from one prison to another and sell and establish plants for conducting and maintaining such industries. Machinery used in an industry which is discontinued and which cannot be used in industries thereafter established, shall be sold for the best price obtainable, due notice of such sale being given to probable purchasers by advertisement or otherwise.

[R. S., pt. IV, chap. 3, tit. II, § 104, as amended by
L. 1889, chap. 382, and L. 1896, chap. 429.

The present law authorizes the superintendent " to change or dispose of the present plants and machinery in said institutions now used in industries which shall be discontinued, and which can not be used in the industries hereafter to be carried on in said prisons, due effort to be made by full notice to probable purchasers, in case of sales of industries or machinery, to obtain the best price possible for the property sold, and good will of the business to be discontinued." This provision is of a temporary nature and was evidently enacted to enable the superintendent to change from the old contract system of prison labor to the system authorized by the constitution of 1895.

It is possible that under the present system it will be necessary for the superintendent to discontinue industries and dispose of manufacturing plants. We have therefore retained the power contained in the present law.]

§ 322. Purchase of machinery and supplies.—The warden of each state prison, with the approval of the superintendent, may procure and maintain machinery, tools, apparatus, and accommodations, and purchase supplies necessary for carrying on the trades and industries in such prison. The amount expended therefor shall not exceed the amount at the disposal of such prison for such purposes.

[R. S., pt. IV, chap. 3, tit. II, § 113, first sentence,
as amended by L. 1889, chap. 382.

The provisions of the present law are as follows:
" § 113. The agents and wardens of the state prisons with the approval of the superintendent of state prisons and the manager or other authorities by whatever name known having charge of the penal institutions of the state are authorized within the ap-

propriations which may be placed at their disposal by the state or by the county supporting such institutions to procure and maintain all necessary machinery, tools, apparatus or accommodations needful for the purpose of carrying on and conducting such trades and industries as may be authorized under the provisions of this act."]

§ 323. **Monthly estimates in relation to manufactures.** — The warden of each state prison, on the first of each month, shall make and forward to the superintendent an estimate in detail of the quantity, quality and cost of materials, machinery, tools and other appurtenances and accommodations required for conducting the industries of the prison and the industrial training and education of the prisoners therein, or which should be contracted for during the next ensuing month. The superintendent may revise such estimate by reducing the quantity and cost or by changing the quality of the articles mentioned therein. He shall deliver the revised estimate to the state comptroller with his certificate annexed, to the effect that he has carefully examined such estimate and that the articles mentioned therein are actually needed for the use of the prison as therein specified. No purchases or contracts on behalf of the state for the industrial purposes of such prison shall be made except for the articles contained in such estimate.

[R. S., pt. IV, chap. 3, tit. II, §§ 112, 114, as amended by L. 1889, chap. 382, and L. 1896, chap. 429, without change.]

§ 324. **Manner of purchasing materials for manufacturing purposes.**—Unless the superintendent shall deem it to be for the best interest of the state to purchase the same in open market, materials to be used in the manufacture of products in a state prison, shall be purchased under a contract executed by the warden thereof. No such contract shall be executed without the approval of the superintendent. Such contract shall be let to the person agreeing to furnish such materials upon terms most advantageous to the state upon his giving satisfactory security for the performance of such contract.

If such materials are to be purchased under a contract, notice shall be given by advertisement daily for not less than two weeks in the state paper at Albany and in at least two newspapers published in the city of New York, that at a time and place therein specified sealed bids will be received for furnishing such materials. Such notice shall state the kind and quantity of materials to be purchased, the time and place of delivery, and such other information as the superintendent shall deem advisable.

All such contracts shall be in writing and signed in triplicate by the parties. One of such triplicates shall be retained by the party agreeing to furnish such materials, one shall be filed with the warden of the prison and one with the superintendent. If the superintendent deems it for the best interests of the state he may reject any or all bids and advertise anew.

[R. S., pt. IV, chap. 3, tit. II, § 113, as amended by
   L. 1889, chap. 382.

The changes made are for the most part verbal. The contract is to be executed in triplicate, instead of in duplicate, as provided by the present law. For comparison we have inserted that part of § 113 from which the above section is derived:

"They shall purchase material in the manner following: All purchases and contracts for the material to be used in the manufacture of goods in the state prisons and other penal institutions of the state shall be made by advertising for sealed proposals (except when in the judgment of the superintendent of state prisons it is for the best interest of the state to purchase the same in the open market). Whenever proposals for furnishing materials have been solicited the parties responding to such solicitations shall be duly notified of the time and place of opening the bids and may be present either in person or by attorney and a record of each bid shall then and there be made. They shall advertise for said proposals or bids daily for at least two weeks in one newspaper published in the city of Albany and two newspapers published in the city of New York specifying the classes and quantity of material required and furnish bidders on demand with printed schedules giving a full description of all of the materials required with date and place of delivery and all other necessary information. The person offering to furnish said materials upon terms most advantageous to the state, and who will give satisfactory security for the performance thereof (in case immediate delivery is not required) shall receive the contract to furnish said material unless the superintendent of state prisons shall deem it to the best interest of the state to decline all proposals and advertise anew."]

§ 325. **Deposit of proceeds of labor of prisoners in banks.**—The warden of each state prison shall deposit in a bank convenient thereto, designated by the comptroller, all moneys received by him as proceeds of the sales of articles manufactured in such prison and of the labor of prisoners therein. No deposit shall be so made, until such bank shall execute and file with the comptroller a bond in a sum, upon the conditions, and with sureties approved by him. Such warden shall deposit such moneys at least once in each week to his credit as such warden.

[R. S., pt. IV, chap. 3, tit. II, § 115, first two sentences and first clause of the third sentence, as amended by L. 1889, chap. 382, without change.]

§ 326. **Weekly statement of deposits.**—The warden of each state prison shall make a weekly statement to the comptroller and the superintendent, showing the amounts received and deposited on account of prison industries, when, from whom and for what received, and the date of such deposits. Such statement shall be certified by the proper officer of the bank receiving such deposits, and shall be verified by the oath of the warden, to the effect that the sum so deposited includes all the moneys received since the time for which the last statement was made, as the proceeds of the sales of articles manufactured in such prison and of the labor of the prisoners therein.

[R. S., pt. IV, chap. 3, tit. II, § 115, part of third sentence, as amended by L. 1889, chap. 382, without change.]

§ 327. **Payment of drafts.**—All moneys so deposited to the credit of the warden of a state prison shall be paid out upon his check or draft countersigned by the comptroller. The comptroller shall not countersign such check or draft, unless it is drawn for the payment of an expenditure included in an estimate made and approved as provided in this article.

[R. S., pt. IV, chap. 3, tit. II, § 115, fourth and fifth sentences, as amended by L. 1889, chap. 382, without change.]

§ 328. **Transfer of deposits to prison fund.**—If the balance on deposit in any such bank shall, at any time, be in excess of the amount needed, in the opinion of the comptroller, for the industrial expenses of a state prison, he shall notify the treasurer of the state and such bank of such excess, and the amount thereof shall be credited to the prison fund and shall not be thereafter payable by such bank, except upon the draft of the state treasurer.

Whenever the warden of a state prison has deposited to his credit as warden, moneys received by him as the proceeds of the labor of prisoners and the sales of articles manufactured by them, that are not required for carrying on the industries of such prison, the superintendent of state prisons may, with the consent of the comptroller, cause such moneys to be drawn from the banks in which they may be, and to be deposited, in such banks as the comptroller may designate, to the credit of the warden of either of the other state prisons, to be used in carrying on the industries in the prison of which such last-named warden is in charge.

[R. S., pt. IV, chap. 3, tit. II, § 115, sixth sentence, as amended by L. 1889, chap. 382, is included in the first paragraph of the above section, without change. The last paragraph is new.]

§ 329. Monthly statements of wardens relating to prison industries.—The warden of each state prison shall render to the superintendent on the first day of each month, a report verified by the oath of the warden, containing a detailed statement:

1. Of materials, machinery or other property purchased during the preceding month and the amount paid therefor.

2. Of the amount expended for other manufacturing purposes during such month.

3. Of materials then on hand to be manufactured or in process of manufacture and of all manufactured products.

4. Of the machinery, fixtures or other appurtenances on hand at such time, for the purpose of maintaining the manufacturing industries in such prison.

5. Of the amount and kinds of work done and the amount of the earnings receivable therefor.

6. Of the amount received by the warden as the proceeds of the labor of the prison during the preceding month.

[R. S., pt. IV, chap. 3, tit. II, § 111, as amended by L. 1889, chap. 382, without change.]

§ 330. **Comptroller's report relating to prison industries.**—The comptroller shall annually, in the month of January, report to the legislature the financial condition of the manufacturing industries of each state prison at the close of the preceding fiscal year. Such report shall state the amount and value of goods manufactured, the amount and value of goods sold and paid for and the sums paid therefor, the amount and value of goods sold and not paid for and the sums due therefor, the amount and value of manufactured goods on hand and the amount and value of unmanufactured material on hand, the amount of money remaining on deposit in banks, such losses as may have occurred during the preceding fiscal year and such other information relating to the manufacturing industries therein, as he may deem important. The warden of each prison shall furnish the comptroller, upon his request, all information necessary to prepare such report.

[R. S., pt. IV, chap. 3, tit. II, § 115, as amended by L. 1889, chap. 382, without change, except that the last sentence is new.]

§ 331. **Superintendent's annual report.**—The superintendent shall include in his annual report to the legislature a statement showing the proceeds of the labor of the prisoners in the several state prisons, and, in detail, the quantity and quality of each class of articles manufactured therein and of the disposition thereof.

[R. S., pt. IV, chap. 3. tit. II, § 104, last sentence, as amended by L. 1889, chap. 382, and L. 1896, chap. 429, without change.]

ARTICLE XVII.

COMPENSATION OF PRISONERS IN STATE PRISONS AND PENITENTIARIES.

Section 340. Compensation of prisoners.

341. Fines of prisoners for misconduct.

342. Disposition of fines.

343. Disbursement of compensation of prisoners.

[General note.—Sections 108-110 of R. S., pt. IV, ch. 3, tit. II, as amended by L. 1889, chap. 382, relating to the compensation and fines of prisoners in state prisons and penitentiaries are included in this article, without change in substance.]

§ 340. **Compensation of prisoners.**—A prisoner confined in a state prison or penitentiary under an indeterminate sentence or who is entitled to a commutation of his sentence for good conduct, as provided in this chapter, shall be allowed compensation for his labor from the amounts received from the sale of articles manufactured in, and the employment of the prisoners of, such institution, by the warden or superintendent thereof. The rate of compensation to each prisoner shall be fixed by such warden or superintendent. The total amount allowed to all prisoners in an institution shall not exceed ten per centum of the amounts so received.

The rate of compensation shall be graded according to the willingness, industry and good conduct of each prisoner and the value of the work performed by him. A prisoner serving a life sentence shall be entitled to the benefit of this section, if his conduct is such as would entitle another prisoner to a commutation of sentence.

If a prisoner shall forfeit any of the time allowed to him as commutation of his sentence for good conduct, by misconduct or violation of the rules and regulations of the institution, there shall be deducted from the compensation allowed him under this section, the sum of fifty cents for each day so forfeited; and a prisoner under an indeterminate sentence shall, in like manner, suffer loss of compensation to the same extent.

[R. S., pt. IV, chap. 3, tit. II, § 108, all except last sentence, as amended by L. 1889, chap. 382, and L. 1896, chap. 429, without change, except that the reference to reformatories is omitted, because reformatories are subject to special provisions relating to compensation, which in effect supersede and modify the provisions of this section.]

§ 341. Fines of prisoners for misconduct.—The warden or superintendent of a state prison or penitentiary may adopt and maintain a uniform system of fines, to be imposed upon prisoners entitled to compensation for their labor, for misconduct or violation of rules and regulations, in the place of other penalties and punishments. The fines imposed upon a prisoner shall be deducted from the compensation credited to him on the books of the institution.

[R. S., pt. IV, chap. 3, tit. II, § 108, last sentence, as amended by L. 1889, chap. 382, and L. 1896, chap. 429, without change.]

§ 342. Disposition of fines.—All moneys deducted as fines from the compensation of prisoners confined in a state prison shall be credited to a special fund and shall be disbursed by direction of the superintendent to aid discharged prisoners who are infirm, indigent or unable to earn a sufficient subsistence after their release. The moneys so deducted from the compensation of prisoners confined in a penitentiary shall be credited to a general fund and be disbursed as directed by the board of supervisors of the county wherein such penitentiary is located or, in the counties of New York and Kings, by the commissioner of corrections in the city of New York.

[R. S., pt. IV, chap. 3, tit. II, § 109, as amended by L. 1889, chap. 382, and L. 1896, chap. 429, without change.]

§ 343. Disbursement of compensation of prisoners.—Upon the absolute discharge of a prisoner, the balance of compensation credited to him upon the books of the penal institution from which he is discharged shall be subject to his draft at his pleasure. Upon the parole of a prisoner from a state prison, he may draw the whole or a part of such balance, at the time and in the manner prescribed by the superintendent. If such prisoner is retaken because of a violation of the conditions of his parole, he shall thereby forfeit a part or the whole of the balance of compensation credited to him. The amount so forfeited shall be disposed of as provided herein for the disposition of fines.

The amount of the balance to the credit of such prisoner may be drawn by him during his imprisonment to aid his dependent relatives or to purchase books, instruments and instruction not supplied to prisoners in his grade, in such institution. Such amount shall not be so drawn by a prisoner confined in a state prison without the certified approval of the superintendent. No part of such amount shall be disbursed for the purchase of food, clothing or ornaments for such prisoner.

[R. S., pt. IV, chap. 3, tit. II, § 110, as amended by
L. 1889, chap. 382.

The changes made are verbal. We have attempted to simplify the language, but have not intended to change the substance of the present law.]

ARTICLE XVIII.

DISCIPLINE AND COMMUTATIONS FOR GOOD CONDUCT.

Section 350. Enforcement of discipline.

    351. Infliction of unusual punishments.

    352. Commutation of sentence.

    353. Rules governing commutations.

    354. Commutation boards.

    355. Monthly report of board to governor.

    356. Allowance of commutation by governor.

    357. Conditions of commutation.

    358. Report of escapes to superintendent of state prisons.

    359. Effect of escapes upon commutations.

Section 360. Commutation of prisoners transferred to the state hospital for insane criminals or to a reformatory.

361. Explanation of commutation law to prisoners.

[General note.—This article includes a revision of existing statutes relating to the discipline and commutation for good conduct of prisoners in state prisons and penitentiaries. The changes made are, for the most part, verbal and are noted at the end of the several sections.]

§ 350. Enforcement of discipline.—The punishments commonly known as the shower bath, crucifix, and yoke and buck shall not be used in a state prison or penitentiary. A keeper, guard or other officer therein shall not inflict blows upon a prisoner, unless in self defence, or to suppress a revolt or insurrection. If a prisoner therein offers violence to another prisoner or to an officer, or injures or attempts to injure the property of such an institution, or attempts to escape therefrom or disobeys or resists any lawful command of the officers thereof, all suitable means shall be used by such officers to defend themselves, to enforce observation of discipline, to secure the person of the offender, and to prevent any such attempt to escape.

[R. S., pt. IV, chap. 3, tit. II, § 87, as amended by
L. 1889, chap. 382, without change.]

§ 351. Infliction of unusual punishments.—If the warden, superintendent, or principal keeper of such an institution deems it necessary, in any case, to inflict unusual punishment in order to produce the entire submission or obedience of a prisoner, he shall confine him in a cell, upon a short allowance, and detain him therein until he shall be reduced to submission and obedience. The short allowance of each prisoner so confined shall be prescribed by the physician, who shall visit such prisoner daily and oftener if required by the warden or superintendent, and examine into the state of his health, until the prisoner is released from solitary confinement and returns to his labor.

[R. S., pt. IV, chap. 3, tit. II, § 88, as amended by L. 1889, chap. 382, without change.]

§ 352. Commutation of sentence.—A prisoner confined in a state prison, or in a reformatory by virtue of a transfer thereto from a state prison, for a term fixed by the court imposing the sentence or the maximum of which is fixed by law, except for a term of life imprisonment, may earn a commutation or diminution of sentence of two months for each of the first and second years, four months for each of the third and fourth years and five months for each subsequent year, and at the same rates for each fractional part of such years. A prisoner confined in a penitentiary under sentence for a term of six months or more, except as an alternative to the payment of a fine, may earn a commutation or diminution of sentence at the same rates. When a prisoner is confined upon more than one conviction, the several terms shall be construed as one continuous term. For the purpose of computing such commutation the term of imprisonment of each prisoner shall begin upon his actual incarceration in such state prison or penitentiary.

A prisoner confined in a state prison for a term, the minimum and maximum of which are fixed by the court imposing the sentence, may earn a like commutation or diminution of sentence based upon the maximum limit of such term.

[L. 1886, chap. 21, §§ 1-3.

Under the present law prisoners confined in penitentiaries are entitled to commutation of sentence, only in case of being sentenced to imprisonment for a term of one year. Commutation for good conduct applied to prisoners sentenced to six months or more would be an aid to discipline. The last sentence is new.]

§ 353. Rules governing commutations.—The superintendent of state prisons shall prescribe and may modify rules governing the allowance or disallowance of commutation to prisoners and shall forward a copy of such rules and of all modifications thereof to the wardens and superintendents of the institutions where prisoners are confined who are entitled to commutations. Such rules shall be strictly followed in all such institutions. A copy of such rules shall be furnished to each prisoner entitled to commutation, upon his reception, and every modification thereof shall be delivered to him as soon as it becomes operative.

[L. 1886, chap. 21, § 6.

Many superfluous words have been omitted, but no intended change has been made.

The present law is as follows:

"§ 6. As soon as practicable after the passage of this act, the superintendent of state prisons shall formulate rules governing the allowance or disallowance of commutation to convicts for good conduct in prison or penitentiary which shall in all cases be strictly adhered to in all the prisons and penitentiaries in this state. These rules may be changed from time to time, if necessary, in the discretion of the superintendent of state prisons, and he shall immediately on their adoption, or of any changes in the same thereafter, cause copies of the same to be forwarded to the agents and wardens of all the prisons, and the wardens or superintendents of all the penitentiaries in this state. A copy of these rules shall be furnished to every convict entitled to the benefits of this act."]

§ 354. Commutation boards.—There shall be a commutation board in each state prison and penitentiary, which, in a state prison, shall consist of the warden, principal keeper and physician thereof, and, in a penitentiary, of the warden or superintendent, the deputy or principal keeper, and the physician thereof or of the persons acting in such capacities. Such board shall apply the commutation rules, and shall meet before the twentieth day of each month, and compute the amount of commutation of prisoners who would be discharged during the ensuing month if full commutation is allowed as fixed by this chapter, and determine the amount which they recommend to be allowed to such prisoners. The board may recommend the withholding of the whole or a part of the allowance of commutation as a punishment for offenses against the discipline of the prison or penitentiary, in accordance with the commutation rules.

[L. 1886, chap. 21, § 7, without change.]

§ 355. Monthly report of board to governor.—The commutation board of each state prison and penitentiary shall make a written report, signed by the members thereof, to the governor, on or before the twentieth day of each month stating:

1. The name and alias of each prisoner who would be discharged during the ensuing month, if full commutation was allowed, the amount of such commutation as fixed by this chapter, and the amount recommended to be allowed.

2. The place at which he was sentenced.

3. A brief description of the crime.

4. The name of the court and the presiding judge thereof.

5. The date of his sentence and reception at the state prison or penitentiary.

6. The term for which he was sentenced and the amount of his fine, if any.

7. The date of his discharge from the prison or penitentiary, if the commutation is allowed.

The form, size and arrangement of such reports shall be fixed by the governor. If the board shall recommend that the commutation for the good conduct of any prisoner be withheld in whole or in part, they shall forward with their report to the governor, their reasons therefor.

[L. 1886, chap. 21, §§ 4, 8, 12, consolidated and rewritten.
Such sections are as follows:
"§ 4. On any day not later than the twentieth day of each month, the agent and warden of each of the state prisons in this state, and the warden or superintendent of each of the penitentiaries in this state, shall forward to the governor a report, directed to him, of any convict or convicts who may be discharged the following month by reason of the commutation of his or her sentence or their sentences in the manner hereinafter provided, which may be written or printed, or partly written and partly printed, which shall be uniform as to size and arrangement, which size and arrangement shall be fixed by the governor, and shall contain the following information, distinctly written, namely: The full name of the convict, together with any alias which he or she may be known to have, the name of the county where the conviction was had, a brief description of the crime of which the convict was convicted, the name of the court in which the conviction was had, the name of the presiding judge, the date of sentence, the date of reception in the prison or penitentiary, the term and fine. the amount of commutation recommended, and the date for discharge from prison or penitentiary, if allowed.

"§ 8. In all cases, however, where the board shall recommend the withholding of the allowance of the whole or any part of commutation for good conduct, they shall forward with their report to the governor their reasons, in writing, for such disallowance, and the governor may, in his discretion, decrease or increase the amount of commutation as recommended by the said board, but he shall not increase the same beyond the amount fixed by this act.

"§ 12. The reports of the various boards for the determination of the amount of commutation for good conduct of convicts in the prisons and penitentiaries of this state to the governor, shall be personally signed by the members thereof."]

§ 356. Allowance of commutation by governor.—Upon receipt of such report, the governor may allow the commutation recommended, or may increase or decrease the same within the limits fixed by this chapter. He shall place the names of the prisoners in the same prison or penitentiary whose terms he may determine to commute, upon one warrant, and forward it to the warden or superintendent of such prison or penitentiary. The prisoners named in such warrant shall be discharged by each such warden or superintendent upon the date mentioned therein, or if such date be Sunday or a public holiday, on the following day.

[L. 1886, chap. 21, §§ 5, 8, 13. Consolidated without change.
The provision authorizing the governor to increase or decrease the commutation is a part of the last clause of § 8. See note to preceding section.]

§ 357. Conditions of commutation.—There shall be annexed to each such commutation of sentence by the governor a condition to the effect, that if any such discharged prisoner is convicted of a felony committed after his discharge and before the expiration of the full term for which he was originally sentenced, he shall be compelled to serve that portion of his original term which was commuted before and in addition to the sentence imposed for such felony. The certificate of a warden or superintendent of a prison or penitentiary, that the period of imprisonment of a convict was commuted, and of the crime and length of term for which such commutation was granted, shall be received as proof of such commutation.

The provisions of this section shall be read and fully explained by the clerk of the prison or penitentiary, to each convict upon his discharge by reason of commutation of sentence.

[L. 1886, chap. 21, §§ 14, 15, 17. Consolidated and rewritten but without change.]

§ 358. Report of escapes to superintendent of state prisons.— The commutation board of each state prison and penitentiary shall investigate each escape or attempt to escape therefrom and examine, under oath, all persons having knowledge of the subject, and reduce their testimony to writing, which shall be signed by such persons. The board shall, at once, make a full written report of all the facts to the superintendent of state prisons, who shall determine whether an escape was made or attempted, endorse his decision upon such report and return the same to the warden or superintendent of the prison or penitentiary, making such report. Such warden or superintendent shall thereupon cause such report and endorsement to be recorded in a book kept for that purpose.

If after such decision there is reasonable ground for believing that injustice has been done to any prisoner, the superintendent of state prisons may order the warden or superintendent of a state prison or penitentiary to re-examine the case and make a new report to him. The proceedings upon such re-examination shall be the same as upon an original examination, and the decision of the superintendent of state prisons shall be rendered in the same manner.

The provisions of this section do not apply to the escape or attempted escape of a prisoner who is not entitled to a commutation of his sentence for good conduct, as prescribed in this article.

[L. 1886, chap. 21, § 10, rewritten but without intended change in substance. We have inserted such § 10 for comparison:

"§ 10. The board hereinbefore provided for to fix the amount of commutation for good conduct shall, immediately on the escape or attempt to escape of any convict, meet and proceed to investigate the said escape or attempt to escape, reduce the testimony of all persons having knowledge on the subject to writing, cause the said persons to affix their signature thereto and make oath to the same before any one of the members of said board, who is hereby authorized and empowered to administer such oath, and false swearing on such examination or in such statement shall be perjury. The said board shall thereupon make a full report in writing, and immediately forward the same to the superintendent of state prisons, who shall thereupon determine whether an escape or attempt to escape was committed, make an indorsement, in writing, of his decision, and return the same to the agent and warden of the state prison, or the warden or superintendent of the penitentiary where the escape or attempt to escape shall have occurred, where the same shall be recorded in a book to be kept for that purpose. But, if from newly-discovered evidence, or other just cause, there is reasonable ground to believe that an injustice has been done to any convict in his or her having been adjudged to have escaped or attempted to have escaped, the superintendent of state prisons may, in his discretion, make an order in writing directed to the agent and warden of the state prison or the warden or superintendent of the penitentiary from which such convict was adjudged to have escaped or attempted to have escaped, requiring that a re-examination of the former adjudication be had, and upon a report to him of such re-examination, he shall proceed to render a decision upon the same. And the proceedings on such re-examination, the decision and the proceedings had thereunder, shall in all respects be conducted in the manner above set forth in this section as upon a first hearing in the matter of an escape or attempt to escape. But the provisions of this section shall not apply to the case of any convict, the length of whose term or terms is less than one year."]

§ 359. Effect of escape upon commutations.—A prisoner serving a term or terms, the whole of which is less than four years, who escapes or attempts to escape, forfeits all commutation for good conduct. If the whole of such term or terms exceeds four years he forfeits for the first escape or attempt to escape, one-half of such commutation and for the second escape or attempt to escape, the whole thereof.

[L. 1886, chap. 21, § 9, rewritten without change.]

§ 360. Commutation of prisoners transferred to the state hospital for insane criminals or to a reformatory.—A prisoner entitled to commutation of his sentence for good conduct who has been transferred to a hospital for insane criminals or convicts or to a state reformatory, pursuant to law, shall be entitled to such commutation notwithstanding such transfer. The medical superintendent of such hospital and the superintendent of such reformatory shall perform the duties of a commutation board for such hospital or reformatory, in respect to the prisoner so transferred, as provided in this article. All the provisions of this article relating to commutation of sentences shall apply to a prisoner so transferred.

[L. 1886, chap. 21, §§ 18, 19, consolidated without change, except in language.

Such sections are as follows:

" § 18. The provisions of this act shall apply to any convict who may have been transferred to the state asylum for insane criminals from either of the prisons or penitentiaries, or from any reformatory of this state to which he or she may have been transferred from any of the prisons or penitentiaries of this state whose sentence or sentences aggregates or aggregate not less than one year. And the medical superintendent of the state asylum for insane criminals may and shall perform any of the acts which may or shall be done by any board mentioned in this act.

"§ 19. The provisions of this act shall apply to any convict who may have been transferred from either of the prisons or penitentiaries to any reformatory of this state whose sentence or sentences equals or equal not less than one year. And the superintendent or chief officer of any reformatory in this state in which any convict may be transferred as aforesaid, may and shall perform any of the acts which may or shall be done by any board mentioned in this act."]

§ 361. **Explanation of commutation law to prisoners.**—Upon the reception within a prison or penitentiary of a prisoner entitled to commutation of his sentence for good conduct, the clerk of the prison or penitentiary shall read and fully explain to him the provisions of this article relating to commutations.

[L. 1886, chap. 21, § 16, without change.]

ARTICLE XIX.

REPRIEVES, COMMUTATIONS AND PARDONS BY THE GOVERNOR.

Section 370. Applications for reprieves, commutations and pardons.

Section 371. Judge or district attorney to furnish facts.

 372. Appointment of person to hear application.

 373. Subpoenas for attendance of witnesses.

 374. Examination of witnesses.

 375. Disbursements.

[General note.—The state constitution, article 4, § 5, authorizes the governor to grant reprieves, commutations and pardons. Existing statutes relating to the exercise of this power are included in this article. It is proposed to repeal §§ 692-695 of the code of criminal procedure. Section 695 is contained in § 371 of this article. Sections 692-694 are not re-enacted as they are a repetition of the provisions of the constitution above referred to.]

§ 370. Applications for reprieves, commutations and pardons.—Reprieves, commutations other than those fixed by the preceding article, and pardons after conviction may be granted by the governor upon applications being made therefor in the form and manner prescribed by him.

[This section is new. See state constitution, art. IV, § 5.]

§ 371. Judge or district attorney to furnish facts.—When application is made to the governor for such pardon, commutation or reprieve, the presiding judge of the court before whom the conviction was had, the district attorney conducting the prosecution, or the district attorney of the county where the conviction was had, in office at the time the application is made, shall without delay supply the governor, at his request, with a statement of the facts proved on the trial, or, if a trial was not had, of the facts presented to the grand jury which found the indictment, and of any other facts relating to the propriety of granting or refusing such pardon, commutation or reprieve.

[Code Crim. Pro., § 695, without change.]

§ 372. Appointment of person to hear application.—The governor may appoint a person as a commissioner to conduct a hearing in a matter pertaining to an application for a pardon, commutation or reprieve. Such commissioner shall receive as compensation not exceeding ten dollars for each day's actual service. Upon the conclusion of such hearing he shall forward to the governor the testimony taken before him.

[L. 1887, chap. 213, first two sentences of § 2, without change.]

§ 373. Subpoenas for attendance of witnesses.—In a hearing upon an application for a pardon, commutation or reprieve, the governor may issue a subpoena or a subpoena duces tecum, to compel the attendance of a witness or the production of necessary books, papers and writings before him or a commissioner appointed by him, at a time and place designated therein. Such a subpoena shall be signed by the governor's private secretary and attested with the privy seal of the state and may be served by any person authorized to serve subpoenas in civil or criminal actions.

[The present law (L. 1887, chap. 213, § 1), authorizes the governor to issue a subpoena to compel the attendance of a witness, expressed in different language but with the same effect as the first sentence of the above section. The last sentence of the proposed section is derived from the first sentence of § 4 of such act.]

§ 374. Examination of witnesses.—The governor or the commissioner appointed by him may examine witnesses on a hearing of any such application and may administer oaths to such witnesses for the purpose of such examination.

The provisions of the code of civil procedure relating to compelling the attendance and testimony of a witness are applicable to a hearing in a matter pertaining to an application for a pardon, commutation or reprieve.

[Sections 3 and 5 of L. 1887, chap. 213, are to be superseded by this section.

Sections 852-869 of the code of civil procedure relate to compelling the attendance of witnesses and provide for conducting the examination. These sections are applicable to proceedings under this article. It is, therefore, unnecessary to re-enact §§ 3 and 5 of such act.]

§ 375. Disbursements.—The disbursements necessarily made in conducting a hearing on an application for a pardon, commutation or reprieve shall be paid upon the approval of the private secretary, out of moneys appropriated for such purposes.

[L. 1887, chap. 213, § 6, without change.]

ARTICLE XX.

MISCELLANEOUS PROVISIONS.

Section 380. United States prisoners.

    381. Expenses of trial of prisoners indicted for offenses in state prisons and reformatories.

    382. Identification of criminals.

    383. Freedom of worship.

    384. Interference with prisoners outside of prison walls; powers of officers to arrest.

    385. Who may visit penal institutions.

§ 380. United States prisoners.—Prisoners convicted in the courts of another state or in the courts of the United States, held without the state, shall not be received in any penal institution of this state. Prisoners convicted in United States courts held within this state and sentenced for a term of one year or more may be received in state prisons and reformatories and maintained and confined therein at the expense of the United States under contracts made with the proper authorities and approved by the superintendent of state prisons. Such prisoners shall not be received in penitentiaries and county jails.

All such prisoners confined in state prisons and reformatories, shall be subject to the provisions of this chapter and the rules and regulations of the institutions in which they are confined, in the same manner and to the same extent as prisoners convicted in the courts of this state.

[R. S., pt. IV, chap. 3, tit. II, § 116, as amended by
L. 1889, chap. 382, and L. 1896, chap. 429.
The changes made are verbal.
The last sentence is new.]

§ 381. Expenses of trial of prisoners indicted for offenses in state prisons and reformatories.—The costs and expenses of the trial of a prisoner indicted and tried for an offense committed while confined in a state prison or reformatory shall be paid by the state. The district attorney of the county in which such trial is had shall make and forward to the state comptroller, a detailed statement, under oath, of the necessary costs and expenses incurred on account of such trial, including the expenses incurred in procuring witnesses to attend before the grand jury and at the trial of the indictment and the amount paid petit jurors for the time occupied by such trial. The comptroller and attorney-general shall examine such statement and strike therefrom all items which are not chargeable to the state under the provisions of this section. The comptroller shall draw his warrant for the amount specified in the statement so corrected in favor of the treasurer of the county wherein such prisoner was indicted and tried, which shall be paid by the state treasurer out of any moneys in the treasury available for such purpose.

[L. 1882, chap. 389, without change.]

§ 382. Identification of criminals.—All prisoners received in a state prison, reformatory or penitentiary, except tramps and those convicted of vagrancy, drunkenness, disorderly conduct and assault in the third degree, shall be measured and described in accordance with the system commonly known as the Bertillon method for the identification of criminals. The superintendent of state prisons shall designate officers of state prisons, reformatories and penitentiaries to make such measurements. He shall prescribe the manner of applying such method of identification and shall make rules and regulations for keeping accurate records of such measurements, and for classifying and indexing the same. Duplicate records of such measurements shall be taken in the manner prescribed by the superintendent of state prisons, one of which shall be retained in the office of the warden or superintendent of such state prison, reformatory or penitentiary and the other shall be transmitted to the superintendent of state prisons to be filed, indexed and classified in his office.

The warden or superintendent of each such state prison, reformatory or penitentiary shall compel a compliance with the provisions of this section and the rules and regulations of the superintendent of state prisons relating to the Bertillon system of identification on the part of the officers of such institutions designated by the superintendent to perform duties relating thereto.

The necessary expenses incurred by the superintendent of state prisons in carrying out the provisions of this section, shall be paid by the state treasurer on the warrant of the comptroller and upon bills approved by such superintendent, out of moneys appropriated for the maintenance and support of the state prisons, but the amount paid therefor shall not exceed the sum of fifteen hundred dollars per annum.

[L. 1896, chap. 440, re-written but without material change, except that it is proposed to except tramps and those convicted of vagrancy, drunkenness, disorderly conduct and assault in the third degree.]

§ 383. Freedom of worship.— Prisoners confined in penal institutions are entitled to the free exercise and enjoyment of religious profession and worship, without discrimination or preference. The rules and regulations of such institutions shall provide for conducting religious services on Sunday and allow private ministration to the prisoners therein in such manner as will best promote and preserve such right. Such prisoners shall be allowed such religious services and spiritual advice and ministration from a recognized clergyman of the denomination or church which such prisoners may respectively prefer, or to which they may have belonged prior to their being confined in such institutions.

If the provisions of this section are violated in a penal institution, the supreme court of the district where such institution is situated may, upon the application of any person feeling himself aggrieved and with at least ten days' notice to the warden, superintendent or keeper of such institution. order a compliance with such provisions.

[L. 1892, chap. 396, so far as it relates to penal institutions is included in this section. It is not proposed to repeal such act.]

§ 384. Interference with prisoners outside of prison walls; powers of officers to arrest.— No person shall interfere with or interrupt the work of a prisoner of a penal institution while employed without the walls thereof, or give or attempt to give intoxicating liquors, beer, ale or any spirituous beverages or any other thing to any such prisoner. No person shall communicate or attempt to communicate with a prisoner while in the custody of an officer of a penal institution outside of the walls thereof without the consent of such officer, or interfere with, disturb or harass any such officer or prisoner. A person violating the provisions of this section is guilty of a misdemeanor. An officer having charge of a prisoner outside of the walls of a penal institution may arrest without a warrant a person committing any such violation in his presence.

[New, except as applied to prisoners employed on the public highway. See L. 1894, chap. 266, § 5.]

§ 385. Who may visit penal institutions.—The following persons may visit at pleasure all penal institutions: the governor and lieutenant-governor, secretary of state, comptroller and attorney-general, members of the legislature, judges of the court of appeals, justices of the supreme court and county judges, district attorneys and every minister of the gospel having charge of a congregation in the city or town in which such penal institution is located. No other person not otherwise authorized by law shall be permitted to enter the rooms of a county jail in which convicts are confined, except under regulations prescribed by the sheriff of the county, or into a penitentiary or state reformatory except under regulations prescribed by the managers or superintendent thereof, or into a state prison except under regulations prescribed by the superintendent of state prisons.

[R. S., pt. IV, chap. 3, tit. III, § 159, without change.
See County Law, § 103.]

ARTICLE XXI.

STATE COMMISSION OF PRISONS.

Section 390. State commission of prisons; appointment, terms of office and compensation of commissioners.

391. Officers and clerical force of commission; compensation.

Section 392. Official seal; meetings of commission.

    393. **General powers and duties of the commission.**

    394. **Visitation and inspection of penal institutions.**

    395. Orders and recommendations of commission after investigation.

    396. Repairs and improvements of county jails and penitentiaries may be directed by the commission.

    397. Annual reports of penal institutions.

    398. Annual report of commission.

[General note.—Chapter 1026 of L. 1895, and the acts amendatory thereof, are included in this article. The changes made are noted at the end of the sections. It is proposed to extend the powers of the commission so that they may enforce their orders and recommendations as to penitentiaries and jails.]

§ 390. State commission of prisons; appointment, terms of office and compensation of commissioners.—There shall continue to be a state commission of prisons. It shall consist of eight members, appointed by the governor, by and with the advice and consent of the senate, one from and to reside in each judicial district of the state. They shall be known as commissioners of prisons and shall hold office for a term of eight years. The commissioners in office when this chapter takes effect, shall continue in office for the terms for which they were respectively appointed.

When the term of office of a commissioner expires at a time other than the last day of December, the term of office of his successor is abridged so as to expire on the last day of December, preceding the time when such term would otherwise expire, and the term of office of each commissioner thereafter appointed shall begin on the first day of January.

Each of such commissioners shall receive as compensation for his time and services the sum of ten dollars per day, for the time actually employed in attending meetings of the commission, and in the performance of official duties by authority or direction of the commission. But the amount paid annually to the members of such commission as compensation shall not exceed the sum of eight thousand dollars. The actual and necessary expenses of each commissioner while engaged in the performance of official duties shall be paid quarterly by the treasurer on the warrant of the comptroller.

[L. 1895, chap. 1026, §§ 1, 8.
Section one of this act specifies the terms of the commissioners first appointed. We have omitted this provision and provided that the commissioners in office when this chapter takes effect shall continue in office for the terms for which they were respectively appointed. This does not alter the terms of office of the commissioners. The provision abridging the terms of the commissioners appointed to succeed those now in office is new and is inserted so that the time for beginning such terms will be uniform with each other and with those of other state commissions and boards. Except as above specified it is proposed to reenact the former law without material change.]

§ 391. **Officers and clerical force of commission; compensation.**—The commission shall annually elect from its members a president. It shall annually elect a secretary and may appoint and remove at pleasure a clerk, at an annual salary of one thousand five hundred dollars, a stenographer and a general office assistant, at an annual salary of one thousand dollars each. The secretary shall keep a record of the proceedings of the commission and perform such duties as are required of him by the commission and by law. He shall receive an annual salary of three thousand dollars. Such commission may appoint inspectors to visit and inspect penal institutions, prescribe their duties and fix their compensation.

[L. 1895, chap. 1026, § 4, all except last clause, without change. The last sentence of the proposed section is new.]

§ 392. Official seal; meetings of commission.—The commission may have an official seal. Every process, order or other paper issued or executed by the commission, may, by its direction, be attested under its seal, by its secretary or by any of its members, and when so attested shall be deemed to be duly executed by the commission. The commission shall meet at least once in three months in its office in the city of Albany. The trustees of public buildings shall set apart suitably furnished rooms for the use of the commission in the state hall or capitol at Albany.

[The first sentence is derived from L. 1895, chap. 1026, § 1, last sentence. The second sentence is new. The remainder of the section is a proposed re-enactment of L. 1895, chap. 1026, § 3.]

§ 393. General powers and duties of the commission.—The commission shall:

1. Make rules and regulations for its meetings, the transaction of its business, and as to the manner of making reports and presenting other matters to it.

2. Visit and inspect all penal institutions.

3. Secure the just, humane and economic administration of all such institutions, except state prisons.

4. Secure the erection of suitable buildings for the use of such institutions, except state prisons, and approve or reject plans for their construction or improvement.

5. Investigate the management of all such institutions, and the conduct and efficiency of the officers charged with such management.

6. Examine into the sanitary condition of the buildings and surroundings of such institutions, and recommend such changes as are required to protect and preserve the health of the inmates.

7. Collect statistics and other information in respect to the property, receipts and expenditures of such institutions and the number and condition of the inmates thereof.

8. Make and enforce uniform rules and regulations applicable to all county jails and penitentiaries, in respect to the separation, labor, treatment and discipline of prisoners confined therein, which rules and regulations shall be printed and distributed to the managers, officers and keepers of such penitentiaries and jails.

9. Ascertain and recommend a system for employing such inmates, which, in the opinion of the commission, may be for the best interests of the public and not in conflict with the provisions of the constitution relating to the employment of prisoners.

[L. 1895, chap. 1026, § 2, and last clause of § 4. Arranged in subdivisions. Under the present law the commission is authorized to "aid in securing the just, humane and economic administration of all institutions subject to its inspection; to aid in securing the erection of suitable buildings for the use of such institutions," etc.

Subdivisions 3 and 4 of the proposed section make the duty of the commission to secure such results.

Subdivision 8 is new. It is inserted for the purpose of authorizing the commission to provide for a uniform system of treatment of prisoners confined in county jails and penitentiaries. The law specifies in detail what may and what may not be done with such prisoners, but there is no power imposed on any board to enforce such provisions. It is suggested that our county jail and penitentiary systems will be benefited by imposing this duty upon the prison commission and by giving them ample power to enforce such provisions and the rules and regulations formulated by them, relating thereto.]

§ 394. Visitation and inspection of penal institutions.—All penal institutions are subject to the visitation and inspection of the commission and of its members, and its secretary and inspectors when authorized by such commission. The commission, or any member thereof, may take proof and hear testimony relating to any matter before it, or before such member, upon any such visit or inspection.

Such commission, any of its members, and its secretary and inspectors, when so authorized shall have full access to the grounds, buildings, books and papers of all such institutions, may question all inmates thereof and require information necessary for the use of the commission from the officers and persons in charge. Such commission may prepare regulations according to which, and provide blanks and forms upon which, the information required by it shall be furnished in a clear, uniform and prompt manner.

The commission may direct an investigation of the affairs and management of a penal institution or of the conduct of the officers and employes thereof, by one or more of its members. The member or members designated to make such investigation may issue subpoenas for the attendance of witnesses and the production of papers, administer oaths and examine persons under oath, and exercise the same powers in respect to such investigation as belong to referees appointed by the supreme court.

Any warden, superintendent, officer or employe of a penal institution who refuses to admit such commission, any of its members, or its secretary or other authorized inspector, for the purpose of visitation or inspection, or refuses or neglects to furnish the information required by such commission, any member thereof, or its secretary, shall be guilty of a misdemeanor, and subject to a fine of one hundred dollars for each such refusal or neglect.

[L. 1895, chap. 1026, §§ 5 and 7, without change.]

§ 395. Orders and recommendations of commission after investigation.—If, upon an investigation into the affairs and management of a state reformatory, jail, penitentiary, or other county prison, or by visitation and inspection thereof, it shall be ascertained that the laws relating to its management and affairs, and the care, treatment and discipline of its inmates, or the rules and regulations of the commission applicable thereto, are being violated, or if it appears that the affairs thereof are being mismanaged, or that its inmates are cruelly, negligently or improperly treated, or inadequate provisions are made for their sustenance, care, supervision or other condition proper for their well-being, the commission may direct the board, superintendent, warden or other officer having charge of any such institution to comply with the law or rules or regulations alleged to have been violated, and to modify the treatment complained of, to change the method of management, or to apply a remedy as specified by them.

If such direction be not followed, an order to the same effect may be issued, signed and attested by the president and secretary of the commission. An application may be made for the approval of such order, to a justice of the supreme court of the judicial district in which the institution complained of is situated, after at least five days' notice to the officer or board having charge of such institution, of the time and place of making such application.

Such order, if reasonable, shall be approved by such justice and when so approved shall be served upon the board, superintendent, warden or other officer having charge of such institution, and a failure to comply with the terms of such order shall be a contempt of court and punished as such.

[This section is new. It provides for the enforcement of the provisions of this chapter and the rules, regulations and orders of the commission by an order of the supreme court. It is provided in § 7 of L. 1895, chap. 1026, that the rights and powers of the commission conferred by such act may be enforced " by an order of the supreme court."]

§ 396. Repairs and improvements of county jails and penitentiaries may be directed by the commission.—If a county jail or penitentiary is:

1. Not of sufficient size to accommodate the prisoners usually committed thereto; or

2. A proper system of ventilation or sanitation is not provided therefor; or

3. Suitable bathing facilities are not furnished to the inmates thereof; or

4. Adequate means are not provided for a separation of prisoners therein as provided by law; or

5. Any other conditions exist which are liable to affect the health and morals of the prisoners confined therein,

The commission may issue a notice, signed and attested by its president and secretary, specifying the defects complained of, in the construction of such jail or penitentiary and requiring the board of supervisors or other authorities, whose duty it is to provide for the improvement or repair thereof, to remedy such defects within a reasonable time specified in such notice. If such jail or penitentiary is located in a county outside of the city of New York, such notice shall be served personally or by mail upon the chairman of the board of supervisors of such county within five days after the board meets in annual session. If such jail or penitentiary is located in the city of New York, such notice shall be served on or before the first of October in any year, upon the mayor, as presiding officer of the board of estimate and apportionment; if the board of supervisors of a county outside of the city of New York, or the board of estimate and apportionment and the municipal assembly in the city of New York, shall fail to comply with the requirements of such notice within the time therein specified, the commission may make an application to the supreme court at a special term thereof, within the judicial district wherein such jail or penitentiary is located, for an order directing the sheriff or other officer or board having charge of such jail or penitentiary to remedy the defects set forth and complained of in such notice. Notice of such application shall be served upon the officers served with the original notice and upon such sheriff or other officer or board.

If it shall appear upon the hearing of such application that defects exist in such jail or penitentiary which should be remedied, the court shall issue its order directing the sheriff or other officer or board having charge of such jail or penitentiary to remedy such defects in the manner and within the time prescribed in such order. Such order shall limit the cost of the alterations, repairs or improvements required to be made thereby. Such sheriff or other board or officer shall thereupon cause such alterations, repairs and improvements to be made, and the expense thereof shall be a charge upon the county or city liable for the support and maintenance of such jail or penitentiary.

[This section is new.]

§ 397. Annual reports of penal institutions.—The warden, superintendent, keeper or other officer having charge of a penal institution shall, on or before the first day of November in each year, report to the commission of prisons:

1. The number of persons confined in the institution under his charge on the preceding first day of October, who are charged

with crime and awaiting trial or the action of a grand jury, and the nature of the crime charged.

2. The number of persons confined therein at such time convicted of crime, and the nature of the crime.

3. The number of persons detained therein at such time as witnesses and as debtors.

4. The term of sentence of each person detained or confined therein during the year ending on the preceding first day of October.

5. The number of persons admitted during such year and the crime for which admitted.

6. The number of discharges and deaths during such year.

7. Such other facts and information as the commission may require.

Such report shall be in the form prescribed by the commission.
[L. 1895, chap. 1026, § 6, rearranged in subdivisions but without change.]

§ 398. Annual report of commission.—The commission shall annually, in the month of January, make a report to the legislature, stating in detail the result of its work during the preceding year, and containing such information relating to penal institutions as it may deem proper. It may, in such report, recommend such changes in the laws as may appear to be to the best interests of such institutions and of the prison system of the state.

[L. 1895, chap. 1026, § 5, last sentence.
The last sentence of the proposed section is new.]

ARTICLE XXII.

LAWS REPEALED; WHEN TO TAKE EFFECT.

Section 400. Laws repealed.

401. When to take effect.

Section 400. Laws repealed.— Of the laws enumerated in the schedule hereto annexed, that portion specified in the third column thereof is repealed.

§ 401. When to take effect.—This chapter shall take effect on the first day of October, eighteen hundred and ninety-nine.

SCHEDULE OF LAWS REPEALED.

Revised Statutes.	Sections.	Subject matter.
Pt. IV., ch. 3, tit. II........	All, except §74	Relating to state prisons.
1840, ch. 25................	All....	Payment to sheriffs for transportation of prisoners.
1847, ch. 460..............	All, except §74	General Prison Law. Superceding R. S., pt. IV, ch. 111, all.
1847, ch. 497..............	All....	Accounts for transportation of prisoners.
1848, ch. 294..............	All....	Amends L. 1847, ch. 460, § 99.
1849, ch. 331..............	All....	Amends L. 1847, ch. 460, § 23.
1854, ch. 240..............	All....	Amends L. 1847, ch. 460,

Laws of	Section.	Subject matter.
1855, ch. 456	All	Amends L. 1847, ch. 460, § 96.
1855, ch. 552	All	Amends L. 1847, ch. 460, § 34, sub. 5; § 58; § 66, subs. 3 and 6; § 83.
1856, ch. 158	All	Sentence of persons between 16 and 21 years.
1857, ch. 94	All	Amends L. 1847, ch. 460, § 65.
1857, ch. 144	All	Insane criminals.
1859, ch. 289	All	Contracts with counties for support of prisoners in penitentiaries.
1860, ch. 399	All	Amends L. 1847, ch. 460, §§ 35, 36, 37, 48, subs. 6 and 9; §§ 50, 109, 156.
1862, ch. 417	All	Commutations; records of prisoners.
1863, ch. 291	All	Clinton prison, appropriation of certain waters for use of.
1863, ch. 415	All	Amends L. 1862, ch. 417, §§ 1, 2, 4, 5.
1865, ch. 584	All	Females in penitentiaries.

Laws of	Section.	Subject matter.
1866, ch. 667.............	All....	L. amends L. 1865, ch. 584, § 4. §§ 2, 3, clothing to prisoners discharged from penitentiaries.
1868, ch. 599.............	All....	Disinfectants for prisons.
1869, ch. 574.............	All....	§§ 1, 2. Females in Syracuse penitentiary. §§ 3-7. Convicts in penitentiaries; clothing to discharged convicts.
1869, ch. 841.............	All....	Removal of convicts from Sing Sing to Albany penitentiary.
1872, ch. 782.............	All....	Amends L. 1847, ch. 460, § 133.
1874, ch. 209.............	All....	Amends L. 1859, ch. 289, §§ 1, 2, 3.
1874, ch. 247.............	All....	Maintenance of prisoners in Onondaga and Kings county penitentiaries.
1874, ch. 451.............	All....	Amends L. 1847, ch. 460, § 34, subs. 1, 15; §§ 40, 48, sub. 10; §§ 61, 64, 69, 74, 77, 1099.

Laws of	Section.	Subject matter.
1875, ch. 25	All	Labor of prisoners in penitentiaries.
1875, ch. 251	All	Contracts for support of civil prisoners.
1875, ch. 529	All	Sentences to penitentiaries in Kings county.
1875, ch. 571	All	Confinement of felons in penitentiaries.
1876, ch. 108	§§ 1, 2	Amends L. 1859, ch. 289, §§ 2, 3.
1877, ch. 172	All	Transfer of female prisoners to penitentiaries.
1879, ch. 471	All	Payments to felons discharged from penitentiaries.
1880, ch. 374	All	Warden of Clinton prison to make certain contracts.
1880, ch. 416	All	Amends L. 1847, ch. 360, §§ 150, 151.
1882, ch. 389	All	Expenses of trial of prisoners in state prisons and reformatories.
1884, ch. 21	All	Convict labor.
1885, ch. 261	All	Management of Albany penitentiary.

Laws of	Section.	Subject matter.
1886, ch. 21	All	Commutations.
1887, ch. 711	All, except §§ 7 and 9	Elmira state reformatory.
1888, ch. 440	All	Amended L. 1847, ch. 460, § 43.
1889, ch. 36	All	Apparatus for execution of convicted criminals.
1889, ch. 382	All, except § 74	Amends L. 1847, ch. 460.
1890, ch. 395	All	Added § 116 to L. 1889, ch. 382.
1890, ch. 559	All	Added § 117 to L. 1889, ch. 382.
1891, ch. 115	All	Amends L. 1885, ch. 490, § 1.
1892, ch. 130	All	Amends L. 1889, ch. 382, § 116, as added by L. 1890, ch. 395.
1892, ch. 587	All	Amends L. 1869, ch. 574, § 3.
1892, ch. 686	§§ 90-103, 183	County law; jails.
1893, ch. 114	All	Amends L. 1869, ch. 574, § 3.

Laws of	Section.	Subject matter.
1893, ch. 306	All	State prison for women.
1893, ch. 386	All	Sale of damaged goods.
1894, ch. 208	All	Amends L. 1847, ch. 460, § 67.
1894, ch. 266	All	Employment of prisoners in state prisons on highways.
1894, ch. 465	All	Amends L. 1847, ch. 460, § 65.
1894, ch. 664	All	Added § 5 to L. 1894, ch. 266.
1894, ch. 737	All	Manufacture of brooms in penal institutions.
1895, ch. 372	All	Amends L. 1875, ch. 571, §§ 1, 3.
1895, ch. 473	All	Amends L. 1847, ch. 460, § 107.
1895, ch. 730	All	Amends L. 1847, ch. 460, § 34.
1895, ch. 761	All	Amends L. 1885, ch. 261, §§ 1-4.
1895, ch. 1026	All	State commission of prisons; powers and duties.
1896, ch. 429	All	Amends L. 1847, ch. 460, §§ 97-109, 112, 114, 116.

Laws of	Section.	Subject matter.
1896, ch. 430..............	All....	Amends L.1895, ch. 1026, §§ 4, 7a, 8.
1896, ch. 440..............	All....	Bertillon system of measurements.
1896, ch. 826..............	All....	Amends County Law, § 93.
1897, ch. 216..............	All....	Amends L. 1847, ch. 460, § 67.
1897, ch. 623..............	All....	Amends L. 1847, ch. 460, § 107.
Code Civil Procedure......	110-119.	Commitment and maintenance of civil prisoners.
Code Civil Procedure......	120-134.	Jails and jail discipline.
Code Civil Procedure......	135-144.	Temporary jails and temporary removal of prisoners from jails.
Code Civil Procedure......	145-159.	Jail liberties and escapes.
Code Civil Procedure......	160-171.	Liability for escape from jail liberties.
Code Civil Procedure......	182, 183, 185, 187- 189....	Duties of incoming and outgoing sheriffs as to prisoners.

Laws of	Section.	Subject matter.
Code Criminal Procedure..	505-509.	Execution of death penalty.
Code Criminal Procedure..	692-695.	Reprieves, commutations and pardons by the governor.

Penal Code Amendments, Relative to the Sentencing of Convicts to State Prisons, Reformatories and Penitentiaries.

[NOTE.— The following amendments to the Penal Code are submitted in connection with the foregoing draft of the Prison law. The principal changes suggested are based upon the proposed adoption of an indeterminate sentence, the maximum or minimum of which are to be fixed by the committing magistrates within the limits prescribed by statute. If a person is convicted of a minor felony and it appears to the magistrate that the person should be given the privilege of earning his release, he may impose a sentence with a low minimum. If the crime is a serious one, the minimum may be fixed so near the maximum that the prisoner will not receive the benefit of a parole.

The new matter is indicated by underlining and the omitted matter is in brackets.]

AN ACT to amend the penal code, relating to the sentencing of convicts to state prisons, reformatories and penitentiaries.

The People of the State of New York, represented in Senate and Assembly, do enact as follows:

Section 1. Title eighteen of the penal code is hereby amended by inserting therein two new sections to be known as sections six hundred and eighty-seven-a, and six hundred and eighty-seven-b, and to read as follows:

§ 687a. Indeterminate sentence defined.— The term "indeterminate sentence," as used in this act, and in any law relating to prisoners in state prisons and reformatories, means a sentence imposed upon a person convicted of a crime the minimum and maximum limits of which, only, are specified.

§ 687b. Indeterminate sentences of convicts to state prisons.— A person over sixteen years of age, who is convicted of a felony in any court of this state and sentenced to a state prison, shall be sentenced thereto under an indeterminate sentence, the minimum of which shall not be less than one year, or, in case a minimum is fixed by law, not less than such minimum, and the maximum of which shall not be more than the longest period fixed by law for which the crime is punishable, of which the offender is convicted. The maximum limit of such sentence shall be so fixed as to comply with the provisions of section six hundred and ninety-seven of this act.

§ 2. Sections six hundred and eighty-eight and six hundred and eighty-nine of the penal code are hereby amended to read as follows:

§ 688. Sentence of second offenders.—A person who, after having been convicted within this state, of a felony, or an attempt to commit a felony, or of petty larceny, or, under the laws of any other state, government or country, of a crime which, if committed within this state, would be a felony, commits any crime within this state, is punishable, upon conviction of such second offense, as follows:

[1. If the subsequent crime is such that, upon a first conviction, the offender might be punished, in the discretion of the court, by imprisonment for life, he must be sentenced to imprisonment in a state prison for life.]

1. If the subsequent crime is such that, upon a first conviction, the offender would be punishable by imprisonment for any term less than his natural life, then such [person] offender shall be

sentenced to imprisonment [for a term not less than the longest term, nor more than twice the longest term, prescribed upon a first conviction.] under an indeterminate sentence, the minimum limit of which shall not be less than the longest term fixed by law as a punishment upon a first conviction of such subsequent crime, and the maximum limit of which shall not be more than twice such longest term.

§ 689. Second offense.—A person, who, having been convicted within this state of a misdemeanor, afterwards commits and is convicted of a felony, must be sentenced to imprisonment under an indeterminate sentence, the maximum limit of which must be for the longest term prescribed for the punishment upon a first conviction for the felony.

§ 3. Section six hundred and ninety-six of the penal code, as amended by chapter six hundred and sixty-two of the laws of eighteen hundred and ninety-two, is hereby amended to read as follows:

§ 696. Convict, when sentenced for life.—When a crime is declared by statute to be punishable by imprisonment for not less than a specified number of years, and no limit of the duration of the imprisonment is declared, the court authorized to pronounce judgment upon conviction may, in its discretion, sentence the offender to imprisonment during his natural life, or [for any number of years not less than the amount prescribed] under an indeterminate sentence, the minimum limit of which shall not be less than the number of years prescribed. [When a crime is declared by any of the provisions of this code to be punishable by imprisonment for not more than a specified number of years, the court authorized to pronounce judgment upon conviction may, in its discretion, sentence the offender to imprisonment for any time less than that prescribed by the provisions of this act.]

§ 4. Section six hundred and ninety-seven of the penal code is hereby amended to read as follows:

§ 697. Sentences; how limited.—When a convict is to be sentenced to imprisonment in a state prison [or a penitentiary,] the court before which the conviction was had must limit the maximum term of the sentence, having reference to the probability of the convict earning a reduction of his term for good behavior, as provided by chapter twenty-one of the laws of eighteen hundred and eighty-six, and assuming that such reduction will be earned, so that the sentence will expire during either of the following months: April, May, June, July, August, September and October. But the provisions of this section shall not apply in the following cases:

1. Where the sentence is to be for the term of one year or less.

2. Where the term of imprisonment for the crime of which the convict was convicted absolutely fixes a single definite period of time.

3. Where a judgment of conviction has been affirmed upon an appeal, and it becomes necessary for the court to impose the same sentence as that originally imposed. The officers of every prison [or penitentiary] are hereby expressly prohibited from taking

into their custody any convict sentenced in violation of the provisions of this section, and any convict so illegally sentenced shall be returned by the sheriff of the county where the conviction was held, to the court, to be resentenced in conformity to the provisions of this section. Provided, that if it shall appear to the officers of any prison [or penitentiary] at the time it is sought to incarcerate a convict therein, that the court which imposed the sentence has adjourned, then it shall be lawful for said officers to receive said convict and hold him in custody until he can be resentenced as herein provided, and the second or resentence shall be deemed to have begun on the date of the convict's reception under his first sentence. The officers of any prison [or penitentiary] shall, in the case of a convict so illegally sentenced to imprisonment therein, immediately notify the court of their action.

§ 5. Section six hundred and ninety-eight of the penal code, as amended by chapter three hundred and seventy-four of the laws of eighteen hundred and ninety-six, is hereby amended to read as follows:

§ 698. Imprisonment of female convict.—Any woman over the age of sixteen years, who shall be convicted of a felony in any of the courts of this state, and sentenced to imprisonment therefor, shall, ([when the sentence imposed is one year or more,] be sentenced to imprisonment in the state prison for women at Auburn. [When the sentence imposed is less than one year, she shall be committed to the county jail of the county where convicted, or to a penitentiary, or to a house of refuge for women.]

§ 6. Section six hundred and ninety-nine of the penal code, as amended by chapter five hundred and fifty-three of the laws of eighteen hundred and ninety-six, is hereby amended to read as follows:

§ 699. Sentence of persons between the ages of sixteen and twenty-one years to county jails and penitentiaries.—Where a male person between the ages of sixteen and twenty-one years is convicted of a felony, [or where] and the term of his imprisonment [of a male convict for felony] is fixed by the trial court at less than one year [or less], the court must direct the convict to be imprisoned in a county penitentiary, [instead of a state prison] or in the county jail located in the county where the sentence is imposed. Whenever a child under the age of fourteen years, is charged with the perpetration of a crime, other than a capital crime, which if committed by an adult, would be a felony, the child shall, in the discretion of the court, be tried as for a misdemeanor, and the court, magistrate or tribunal before whom such trial is held, shall impose the penalty as prescribed by law in the case of misdemeanors.

§ 7. Section seven hundred of the penal code is hereby amended to read as follows:

§ 700. Sentence to reformatories of persons between sixteen and thirty years of age.—A male between the ages of sixteen and thirty years, convicted of felony, who has not theretofore been convicted of a felony [crime, punishable by imprisonment in a state prison] may, in the discretion of the trial court be sentenced to imprisonment in the [New York State Reformatory at] Elmira Reformatory, or the Eastern Reformatory at Napanoch when completed and ready for occupancy, to be there confined under the provisions of law relating to such reformatories. Such imprisonment may be terminated by the managers of the reformatory to which such person is sentenced, as authorized by the prison law, but shall not continue for a longer period than the maximum term provided by law for the crime of which the prisoner was convicted.

§ 8. Sections seven hundred and three and seven hundred and four of the penal code are hereby amended to read as follows:

§ 703. *Imprisonment in county jail or state prison.*—No person shall be sentenced to imprisonment in a penitentiary or county jail for a term of more than one year. Where a person is convicted of [a crime, for which the punishment inflicted is imprisonment for a term of one year, he may be sentenced to and the imprisonment may be inflicted by confinement either in a county jail, or in a penitentiary or state prison. No person shall be sentenced to imprisonment in a state prison for less than one year.] a misdemeanor and sentenced to imprisonment therefor, such imprisonment shall be for a term of not more than one year in a penitentiary or county jail.

§ 704. *Imprisonment in state prison.*—No person shall be sentenced to imprisonment in a state prison for a term of less than one year. Where a person is convicted of a felony, [crime for which the punishment inflicted is imprisonment for a term exceeding one year, or is sentenced to imprisonment for such a term] and sentenced to imprisonment therefor, he shall be confined in a state prison at hard labor for not less than one year. But this and the last two sections shall not apply to a case where special provision is made by statute as to the punishment for any particular offense or class of offenses or offenders, nor to the cases specified in section six hundred and ninety-eight, six hundred and ninety-nine, seven hundred and seven hundred and one.

§ 9. Section seventy-four of chapter four hundred and sixty of the laws of eighteen hundred and forty-seven, as amended by chapter three hundred and eighty-two of the laws of eighteen hundred and eighty-nine, and section nine of chapter seven hundred and eleven of the laws of eighteen hundred and eighty-seven are hereby repealed, but the repeal of such sections shall not affect any action heretofore taken thereunder or lessen or in any way affect the term of imprisonment of prisoners confined in a state prison or the Elmira Reformatory and sentenced thereto prior to the taking effect of this act.

§ 10. This act shall take effect October first, eighteen hundred and ninety-nine.

www.ingramcontent.com/pod-product-compliance
Lightning Source LLC
Chambersburg PA
CBHW021841230426
43669CB00008B/1045